D0913168

The Power of Followership

The Power of Followership

How to Create Leaders People Want

to Follow and   Followers Who

Lead Themselves

Robert E. Kelley

CURRENCY   DOUBLEDAY
New York London Toronto Sydney Auckland

A Currency Book
PUBLISHED BY DOUBLEDAY
a division of Bantam Doubleday Dell Publishing Group, Inc.
1540 Broadway, New York, New York 10036

Currency and Doubleday
are trademarks of Doubleday, a division of
Bantam Doubleday Dell Publishing Group, Inc.

"A Worker Reads History" from *Selected Poems*, copyright 1947 by Bertolt Brecht and H. R. Hays and renewed 1975 by Stefon Brecht and H. R. Hays, reprinted by permission of Harcourt Brace Jovanovich, Inc.

Design by Richard Oriolo

Library of Congress Cataloging-in-Publication Data
Kelley, Robert Earl.
The power of followership : how to create leaders people want to follow, and followers who lead themselves / Robert Kelley. — 1st ed.
p.   cm.
Includes bibliographical references and index.
1. Leadership.   I. Title.
HD57.7.K45   1992
658.4'092—dc20   91-40914
                                                          CIP

ISBN 0-385-41306-8

5   7   9   10   8   6   4

To Lauren and Luke
—and to all the other followers
and leaders of the future.

Contents

Preface

This book is about what it feels like to be a follower and how to become a better one. Followers are not all the same. Some merely join, adding their names to the membership list and doing nothing more. Others collaborate with leaders to further some goal in which they believe—a social cause, a creative idea, a new product, a special service, a worthy person. With these followers, new companies take hold and prosper, candidates get elected, and new religions spread across the land. This book details how these active intelligent followers make these dreams happen.

My research is based on several sources. First, I conducted surveys of over seven hundred people, soliciting their views on followership and leadership. Those surveyed are an average thirty-seven years of age, have thirteen years of work experience, and reported to nine different managers over the course of working for three separate companies. They represent over twenty industries. I also interviewed some of these people to obtain richer information and personal anecdotes. Some agreed to be identified; others requested confidentiality. I have honored those requests, omitting identifying information or using pseudonyms when necessary, while preserving the accuracy of their views.

I also presented followership concepts during workshops for many institutions, including the following companies: Bell Laboratories, Hewlett-Packard, IBM, Mellon Bank, Standard Register, AT&T, Bellcore, Pillsbury, Holiday Inn, Upjohn, McKesson, Southwestern Bell, Manufacturer's Hanover, Intel, McCormick and Dodge, Lanier, Northern States Power, PC Week, Alcoa, GTE, U.S. West, Sohio Amoco, and Prudential.

I also presented to these associations: American Paper Institute, Institute of Management Studies, American and Canadian Societies of Association Executives, Alliance of American Insurers, American Society of Training and Development, Council of Oregon School

Administrators, and the Pharmaceutical Manufacturers Association.

The over 1,000 people in these workshops provided input and helped hone the concepts for this book in our give-and-take sessions.

Since 1985 I have taught a course, "Followership and Leadership for Professional Effectiveness," in the Industrial Management Program at the Graduate School of Industrial Administration of Carnegie-Mellon University. The students researched and tested the material for academic soundness and applicability to their own lives. We also were fortunate to have followers and leaders from all walks of life—business, government, religion, philanthropy, education, the law, cultural associations—visit our class. These visitors freely shared their time and experiences as followers and leaders. They included: Anthony J. Bevilacqua, Cardinal, Diocese of Philadelphia; Doreen Boyce, Director, Buhl Foundation; Paul Brophy, Vice-Chair, Enterprise Foundation; Rosemarie Cibik, Superintendent, Pittsburgh Catholic Schools; Richard Cyert, President, Bosch Institute, and former President, Carnegie Mellon University; Ralph Dickerson, Director, United Way of New York; Mary Louise Fennel, President, CEO Consultants, and former President, Carlow College; Elsie Hillman, Chair, Republican National Party; Hydie Houston, Associate Pastor, East Liberty Presbyterian Church; Carol Hymowitz, Pittsburgh Bureau Chief, *Wall Street Journal;* Bill Isler, EVP, Family Communications, Inc.; Barbara Lazarus, Associate Provost, Carnegie-Mellon University; Howard (Pete) Love, former CEO, National Intergroup; Carol Mansmann, Federal Judge, Third Circuit Court of Appeals; Dave Matter, Director of Development, Oxford

Development Company; Joe Mistick, Executive Secretary, Mayor of Pittsburgh's Office; Douglas Nowicki, Arch-Abbot, St. Vincent's Priory; Dennis O'Connor, President, University of Pittsburgh; Robert Pease, Former Executive Director, Allegheny Conference on Community Development; Jim Roddey, Managing Partner, Allegheny Media; Fred Rogers, Creator, *Mister Rogers' Neighborhood;* Dan Rooney, Owner, Pittsburgh Steelers; Herb Simon, University Professor, Carnegie-Mellon University; Nate Smith, Founder, Operation Dig/ Careers Inc.; Lorene Vinski, Assistant to President, The Carnegie; Dean George Werner, Bishop, Trinity Cathedral; Bill White, CEO, Bell & Howell; Bob Wilburn, President, The Carnegie; Lynn Williams, President, United Steelworkers of America.

I have also had the opportunity to interview and observe, firsthand, leaders and followers during the course of my eighteen years as a consultant. My clients include some of America's best-known companies (such as Alcoa, AT&T, Hewlett-Packard, Pillsbury, and Merck), government agencies (such as the Treasury Department and the Federal Home Loan Bank Board), and not-for-profit organizations (such as Stanford Research Institute and the Texas School for the Deaf). Several clients encouraged me to explore my concepts of followership and leadership inside their companies during the past ten years. In particular, Bell Labs gave me access to over six hundred professionals and managers who studied and applied the concepts on the job. They were a fertile and rewarding testing ground.

Finally, I used myself as a research tool. I personally have experienced the joys and difficulties of the follower role. I have benefited from some great leaders, and suf-

4

fered under the yoke of mediocre bosses. As a leader, I know what I admire in my followers and what drives me to distraction. As an author, I tried to temper my experiences with research data, critical review by others, and professional integrity. Nonetheless, I did not ignore my own thoughts and reactions. I believe they are valid in themselves, and validated when they resonate with those of others.

These four sources—research, teaching, consulting, and self—form the basis of this book. But it is by no means exhaustive. My purpose is not to teach you everything you need to know about followership. Rather, I simply want you to think about followership and to share my experience as to *how* to think about it. Directional rather than definitive, the real value is in helping shift the spotlight toward followership as *the* important phenomenon to study if we are to understand why organizations succeed or fail.

Warning: Leadership

May Be Hazardous

for You

Consider these three astonishing observations about leaders and followers:

- Leaders contribute on the average no more than 20 percent to the success of most organizations.

- Followers are critical to the remaining 80 percent.
- Most people, however impressive their title or salary, spend more time working as followers than as leaders. That is, we spend more time reporting to people rather than having people report to us.

Why, given these facts, do people tend to value leaders and undervalue followers? Why do we refuse to appreciate that followers are *us?*

This book is about the power of followers, which has long been unrecognized. In particular, it is about those followers who are exemplary, who are living lives of productivity and contentment which many leaders dream about, who are making it possible for organizations to thrive. Who are these followers and what can we learn from them about how to become stronger in nonleadership positions? But this book also is for leaders. They can read it to see how they look from the other side of the mirror.

The nineties will be the decade of followers. On a global level, hundreds of thousands of Soviet, Eastern European, and African citizens have exercised the power of followership to reclaim control of their countries and their lives. At work, we see increased emphasis on teams, collaboration, employee ownership, and grass-roots movements in the office and on the factory floor.

While followers are constantly getting stronger, leadership is growing weaker. I see resentment building toward the leadership aristocracy who get astronomical pay, perks, and golden parachutes—all while downsizing the rank and file. Most of us feel less need for leadership with strong authority. Also, we are wary of charismatic leaders. We follow to the fullest when leadership is based on expertness or an admirable goal, not because of a title or organizational status.

If there is anything the nineties have already taught us, it's that most people are both leaders and followers. The roles of followers and leaders are no longer as clearly demarcated as they used to be. We need to acknowledge both parts of ourselves. Emphasizing leadership to the exclusion of followership breeds a single-minded conformism.

Witt Stephens, an investment banker from Arkansas, captures the danger of this single-minded pursuit in a story of a trail made by a calf three hundred years before. He described how the trail turned into a path, as dogs and sheep walked in the calf's footsteps. Behind them were people who complained about the winding path but came along anyway. As Stephens says, the path became a lane, then a road, then a village street, then a thoroughfare, then the central street of a renowned metropolis.

> So people two centuries and a half
> Trod in the footsteps of that calf.
> A hundred thousand people were led
> By one calf near three centuries dead.
> For we are prone to go it blind
> Along the calf-paths of the mind
> And work away from sun to sun
> To do what other people have done.

In writing this book, I have tried to keep off the calf-path of leadership to discover what I could about the path of followership. This path is one that's been walked by Aristotle, Thomas Jefferson, Jane Addams, and Alfred Adler—people known as leaders but who proved themselves as followers first and foremost. They were so effective at followership that their peers encouraged them to take on leadership responsibilities.

This book is a work in progress, not a completed study. It is part research, part journalism, part essay. It documents what I have learned over seven years, but there is still much to learn. Compared with the 2,500 years of research in leadership, followership research has just started. You could view this book as the diary of the beginning stages of a 2,500-year research journey into followership. Much still awaits discovery.

1. If the People

Will Lead, the Leaders

Will Follow

In the years since I began researching this book, I have had the following conversation many times. A friend, a stranger sitting next to me on a plane, an executive, or a journalist will ask, "What are you working on?"

"Followership," I say.

"What? Run that by me again."

"Followership—the flip side of leadership," I explain.

"Oh, you mean the people who need to be told what to do. The sheep?"

"No, I mean the people who know what to do without being told—the people who act with intelligence, independence, courage, and a strong sense of ethics. I'm interested in what separates exemplary followers from those who perpetuate the negative stereotypes. I believe the value of followers to any organization is enormous.

"Without his armies, after all, Napoleon was just a man with grandiose ambitions."

My journey into followership began as a flirtation. While researching leadership, I saw limitations in the myth of leadership. Leadership has been exalted for over 2,500 years, so my task was not an easy one. Yet one day a blinding flash of the obvious hit. I realized that few people had studied followers since all the attention was focused on leaders. When people did study followers, they simply asked for their views about leaders. The prevailing assumption was that followers had nothing of interest to say about themselves.

What began as a casual flirtation has become a seven-year study of followership and leadership. I have now dramatically changed my views of power, hierarchy, and the value of ambition as a correlate of success. I have concluded that followership is just as important as leadership, sometimes more important. I have felt the impact of followership's wisdom on my own life.

But I get ahead of myself. Let me take you back to my days in the leadership field, when I too thought negatively about followers, if I thought about them at all.

The Myth of Leadership

There is a story of the drunk who lost his house keys during a midnight pub crawl. On his hands and knees under a lamppost, he searched the same ground over and over. After a while, he walked to the next lamppost and repeated his search. A passerby asked if he dropped his keys near a lamppost. The drunk said, "No." "Then why do you keep searching under lampposts?" the passerby queried. "Because, that's where the light is," responded the drunk.

We have become so mesmerized by the spotlight on leaders that we grow blind to the possibility that the keys to understanding organizational success lie somewhere in the shadows.

The most important shadow, I became convinced, is followership. Followers determine not only if someone will be accepted as a leader but also if that leader will be effective. Effective followers are critical for a leader's or an organization's success.

In 1841, the English philosopher Thomas Carlyle published his book *On Heroes, Hero-Worship, and the Heroic in History*. In it he put forth his theory of the "great man" as prime mover of history and change. Carlyle held that great people have the intellectual ability to pierce through the oppressive humdrum of everyday life to reveal its underlying significance. They create the values by which everybody else exists. Their fitness to rule justifies their claim to obedience and excuses their excesses. Carlyle came close to asserting that might makes right, and his cult of the leader-hero influenced proponents of authoritarian or autocratic organizations.

Since Carlyle, most modern institutions focus on and support leadership. Our educational system, management training programs, and best-selling business books all push leadership as *the* answer, *the* aspiration.

For example, former Stanford University president Donald Kennedy declared that his university's central purpose is to train new leadership for society. "We do so out of faith that their capacity for wise and compassionate leadership is the best possible guarantee of the survival of everything we think is important." I doubt if any university sees itself differently.

Like most people studying leadership, I too thought the universe of achievement, change, and success revolved around leadership. In a society raised on sports heroes, G.I. Joe and Barbie dolls, comic-strip adventurers like Batman and Wonder Woman, as well as legendary figures like Joan of Arc, Abraham Lincoln, and Gandhi, the hero-leader is a cultural icon blazed into our national psyche.

As I studied leaders closely, however, I gradually became uneasy. A modern "cult of leadership" had emerged among executive researchers, journalists, and consultants. In many instances, the cult was overawed by their subjects. Whether CEOs, elected government officials, entrepreneurs, labor leaders, or Nobel laureates, these subjects had power, money, and fame. They could grant or block access to interviews or data. They controlled consulting projects. They could give jobs.

They could, and often did, dictate the terms of any interactions.

CEOs especially held absolute power. While others' opinions of events received critical scrutiny and required cross-checking by multiple sources, leaders' statements were accepted at face value. Seldom were peers or subordinates asked to verify the leader's views. Much of the writing about leadership became no more than *People* magazine platforms for leaders to reminisce, preach, or revise history. Mistakes, personality problems, and damage to others were left out of the record, glossed over, or made to appear virtuous, like "Sure I was one mean SOB, but that's what it took to stay on top." What resulted was not really scholarship or journalism, but collusion in mythmaking.

My uneasiness led me to start questioning what I have come to call "the myth of leadership." All this would have been pretty harmless if the subject matter was sports figures or movie stars. If we set aside the Walter Mittys, few adults hold fantasies or shape their daily lives around these manufactured legends. But millions of managers, workers, and students are fed the leadership myths and take actions based on them. In turn, their actions have an impact on other people and their organizations, for better or worse.

Warren Bennis, a respected leadership guru and best-selling author, declares that a leader:

- Innovates.
- Is an original.
- Develops.
- Focuses on people.
- Inspires trust.

- Has a long-range perspective.
- Asks what and why.
- Has an eye on the horizon.
- Originates.
- Challenges the status quo.
- Is her or his own person.
- Does the right thing.

He says there are ten actions common to leaders coping with change and forging a new future:

- Leaders manage the dream.
- Leaders embrace error.
- Leaders encourage reflective back talk.
- Leaders encourage dissent.
- Leaders possess the Nobel factor (optimism).
- Leaders understand the Pygmalion effect in management.
- Leaders have the Gretzky factor (i.e., a certain touch).
- Leaders see the long view.
- Leaders understand stockholder symmetry.
- Leaders create strategic alliances and partnerships.

This is just one author's view. While few people dispute Bennis' understanding of leadership, every other leadership guru has his own lists and formulas. Put end to end, these lists present a staggering challenge to a would-be leader.

Who, I ask myself, can possibly master one or two items from any of the lists, let alone an entire list? The myth defines leadership in such a narrow way that we mere mortals can never hope to fit the bill, even though we are spurred on to try. The leaders in these books and programs are portrayed as role models embracing and epitomizing every characteristic in every list.

It is possible, we're told. After all, we got it straight from the leaders' mouths.

This view of leadership is a romantic illusion. People like that don't really exist, at least not in corporate America. We might want them to exist, or we might like to think of ourselves as having those qualities. But do you really know anyone who has all those qualities? Forget all the hype you've read about the PR icons, like Lee Iacocca, Jack Welch, or Ted Turner. Think about real people in leadership positions that you know.

I happened to meet and observe firsthand a few of these leaders worshipped in the best sellers. None really measure up to their aura. I see two-faced people praised for their integrity. I see huge halo effects where a leader truly gifted in strategic thinking is then presumed to have skills that she or he does not possess, such as passion or integrity. I also encounter effective leaders who are low on vision, communications, or the other skills on these lists. Yet they still succeed.

Something is askew.

After 2,500 years of research, and 10,000 published leadership studies and endless best-selling books, we still don't know how to produce leaders. No model of leadership has been able to predict reliably which people will be effective leaders. No business school has come up with a surefire way to turn them out. The only advice from the "myth" is to "be like them."

Two hundred years ago, about 3 million people populated what was to become the United States of America. From that tiny population, no fewer than ten or eleven gifted leaders emerged: Jefferson, Washington, Franklin, Adams (John and Samuel), Madison, Hamilton, Paine, Hancock, Lee, and Henry. Yet with 240 million Americans alive today, how many world-class leaders do we have? Why, with eighty times more people, can we not produce ten world-class leaders, let alone 800 of them? Could it be that our country's founders did not have to suffer the yoke of the leadership myth? They probably did not worry about their leadership ability or whether they measured up to some impossible standard. They could just be who they were and do what was needed, without worrying about leading or following.

This notion of the "perfect" leader is a relatively recent phenomenon. Perfection has not always been a prerequisite of effective leadership. The Greek god Zeus, after all, was slovenly, argumentative, and petty. Winston Churchill, the brilliant orator in Britain's time of need, was socially obnoxious, insulting hosts and guests alike.

Leaders possess a collection of traits—some that are praiseworthy, others that are not so admirable. They are far from perfect; all leaders have flaws. We do them and ourselves a disservice when we only acknowledge the positive and then expect perfection. They feel the pressure to live up to an image which they do not fit. We become disappointed when the real person emerges.

I was left with a chilling question: What have we done to ourselves by creating and perpetuating the myth of leadership?

The High Cost of Leader Worship

Worse than the leadership myth's debilitating effect on potential leaders is what it does to the followers. At a minimum, the leadership myth entices people to let down their defenses in the presence of leaders. When the leader's flaws are covered up, followers may place unwarranted trust in the leader simply because of the position or aura. People set themselves up for potential abuse in ways they otherwise would not do.

As one of Jim Bakker's PTL congregation reported bitterly, "He was our minister, our shepherd. We entrusted our life savings into his hands. Instead of safekeeping it for our retirement home at Heritage Land, he squandered it on air-conditioned doghouses."

A more troubling effect is the powerlessness felt by followers. I have consulted to dozens of troubled companies in the past five years. Some have poor product quality. Others are in a corporate malaise as competitors win market shares. The most common complaint I hear is that the corporate leaders are ineffective or that a leadership vacuum exists. The message is that it is the leaders' responsibility to get everyone out of the hole. Average corporate citizens do not view themselves as active participants in the process. The "hero" leadership myth releases them from their responsibility.

In an international electronics company, workers became very dependent on their extremely competent department head for decision making and strategy. Then the leader got hit by a car and was hospitalized for over a month. For the first week, the team func-

19

tioned well because they were completing assignments given to them prior to the accident. In the middle of the second week, they went into a panic. They didn't know what to do next, nor could they figure it out. During an impromptu team meeting, they sat sullenly, each looking to the others for some direction. After squirming for thirty minutes, they found their solution. "What would Joan [the department head] want us to do next?"

This utter dependency is the unfortunate downside of the leadership myth. Not only does it strip people of the power they inherently possess; it also opens the door for abuses of that dependency. In the tradition of Carlyle, some "hero" leaders come to believe they are better than their subordinates and above the rules that govern them. Their power lust emerges in small ways, like John Kennedy demanding to be called Mr. President by his siblings. Or it can become bigger than life, like Hitler's extermination of the Jews. Once society tips the power equation in favor of the myth, it can quickly turn into a tyranny.

To expose the myth is to help us utilize everyone's full talents and our ability to succeed. Leadership can take us only so far. Our societal assumptions about its potency far outstrip reality. Several research studies have examined just how much of a difference leadership makes. That is, after controlling all the other variables, what is the leader's contribution to organizational outcomes? The conclusion: *The leader's effect on organizational success is only 10 to 20 percent.* True, this is still a large effect for only one individual, but as Walter Kiechel of *Fortune* observed, "It may be enough in some competitive situations but it's no revolution."

Followership is the real "people" factor in the other

80 to 90 percent that makes for great success. Without followers, little gets done; with them, mountains get moved. By sheer numbers alone, followers represent the bulk and substance of any enterprise.

Fundamentally, we must begin to see that the errors of leadership are better overcome and the triumphs of history are better achieved by engaging everyone's heroism rather than waiting for some improbable hero to emerge.

Countries of Followers

As I pondered the "triumphs of history," my perspective turned to the follower's role. Rather than accept Carlyle's assumption that leaders are the makers of history, I looked for what the followers did—together and alone—to make history happen.

One night, I found myself in a hotel room with nothing to read but business reports. Wanting to escape from work, I searched for a diversion. I flipped through the room service menu and skimmed the cable television movie guide.

Then I came upon the one reading staple in every hotel room—the Bible. It struck me that major religions, whether Buddhism, Hinduism, Judaism, Islam, Christianity, or any other, are fertile grounds for examining followership and leadership. No one disputes that Buddha, Abraham, Mohammed, and Jesus were great leaders. The religions they founded shaped history. But what of their followers?

As I scanned the New Testament, my thoughts turned to Jesus and Christianity. I tried to picture soci-

21

ety at the time of Jesus' emergence into public life. Israel and its leaders found themselves in a semi-chaotic state. Political radicals, in the tradition of the Maccabees, called for an armed uprising against the Romans. Religious radicals demanded the overthrow of popular dogmas. The social have-nots warred with their rigid religion and gathered around self-appointed prophets, like John the Baptist, who claimed the world was coming to an end and that the Messiah was at hand. This was an uncertain, tense period, sometimes bringing Jewish society to a halt for days at a time.

Jesus and his followers represented one of many newly emerged splinter sects, by no means the largest. Yet why did his survive, flourish, and come to dominate the Western world? He lived only for thirty-three years and participated in public life for only three of those. Other than choosing his twelve apostles (and, some believe, making a mistake with one of those), Jesus shows little evidence of organizational abilities. And, after all, only so much can be done in three years.

I thought of his followers and the role they played. With the exception of Paul (who was not an original apostle but a later convert), very little is said about them. But if they did not do anything worth mentioning, how did this religion flourish? Who decided what got written down and who would do the writing that now comprises the New Testament? Who decided what teachings would be passed on and who would do the teaching? Who spread the religion from Jerusalem to Rome, Antioch, North Africa, Asia Minor, and the Middle East? Who decided who would be accepted into the new religion? Who built the catacombs and ran the meetings? Who collected the money and doled it out? Who designed the organizational structure that kept this far-flung enterprise unified? Which follower climbed out of the catacombs and said, "If we convert Emperor Constantine's mother to our religion, then we'll never have to go back into the catacombs"? Who had the vision of becoming the dominant religion? Is the leader a "prime mover" at all, or only a follower?

Jesus' followers—these unsung heroes—did a lot of work that made the difference. Without them, Jesus would have been like many of his contemporaries, just another "voice in the wilderness." With them, he changed the course of history.

This is the issue Tolstoy grappled with in *War and Peace*. Documenting how Napoleon ravaged Europe and prepared to invade Russia, Tolstoy asks: Is Napoleon really a leader? Or is he someone who noticed that history was already in the making and put himself in the forefront?

Tolstoy attacked historians' practice of fixing responsibility for what occurs in life onto "great people" and endowing them with heroic virtues after the fact. He reasoned that the actions of the so-called makers of history depend on the actions of countless other people —both before and after the leader acts. For Tolstoy, the principles of rightness, justice, and freedom are deeply seated within the lives of ordinary people. The yearning for and expression of these principles motivate countless people to take action. This, not great men and women, determines history.

Lenin, an avid reader of Tolstoy, often proclaimed that he was not the father of the Communist revolution. What he did was to understand how the Russian society was already changing. He then articulated those changes and rode the wave like a surfer.

In the creation of the United States of America,

much credit is given to the Founding Fathers, especially Washington and Jefferson. Did these men cause the American Revolution or was it already happening? The Boston Tea Party appears to have had at least as much effect as the Declaration of Independence.

John Adams confirms this viewpoint. He saw the Revolutionary War as not really revolutionary at all. In reflecting later upon the events that transpired between the British Empire and the colonies during the twelve years prior to the war, he stated, "The revolution was complete, in the minds of the people, and the union of the colonies, before the war commenced in the skirmishes of Concord and Lexington on the 19th of April, 1775."

My hunch is that the representatives to the Constitutional Convention did not view themselves as separate from or better than their neighbors. They understood that they were not prime movers, but participants in changing events. After all, the U.S. Constitution begins with "We, the people," not "We, the leaders."

We are a nation of followers. The United States is a two-hundred-year-old experiment in the belief that common people like you and me—the followers, if you will—believe enough in ourselves to govern ourselves. The spirit of American democracy elevates and celebrates the role of the follower. As a nation, we believe that leaders are accountable to the followers and that followers will determine whether leaders will hold their positions. We have built a country that succeeds (and occasionally fails) by the quality of followership.

Viewing history from the eye of the follower rather than the lens of the leadership myth allowed me to focus on present-day leadership research with a different perspective. I questioned not only whether our peculiar idolatry of leadership was true but also whether leadership really made "the" difference. Tolstoy, Lenin, and Adams make a strong case that history is well into the making before most leaders arrive, and will occur with or without their help.

Finding the Follower Within Us

My first task was to understand what followership is. In *Journey to the East,* Hermann Hesse portrays a group on a mythical journey. The main character, Leo, is a servant and is viewed as such by the group. He does the cooking, the cleaning, and other menial chores. The journey is buoyed by Leo's good spirits. The journey proceeds well until Leo vanishes. The group, it turns out, cannot continue on its own without their servant and supposed follower, Leo. The journey is abandoned.

Some people interpret Hesse to mean that Leo, although a servant, was in reality the journey's leader. The conclusion is that without leadership, everything fails.

I interpret Hesse's story differently. To me, Leo is the quintessential exemplary follower, the kind of person that no leader or group can succeed without. Leo knew what it took for the journey to proceed. He willingly did the tough work without any glory. He did not demand the limelight or constant praise. Leo was content with his role as servant. His departure provides a startling contrast to the lack of followership skills in the other group members. Without effective followership, as Leo displayed, organizations and leaders fail.

To understand the Leos better, I began by asking people in followership positions about being a follower. What was it like? Why did they do it? Were some ways of following better than others? Did they like to follow or did they really want to be the leader? What was their day-to-day life like? What did people think of them and their followership style?

As one software developer revealed, "I've been a follower all my life. It is simply the role I prefer to play. I'm considered one of the best computer jocks in this company. But I have no desire to lead people. I don't care to expend my energy trying to get people to do what I want them to do. I simply turn out great software that people want to buy. So do all the computer hackers sitting along this corridor. Now you tell me: Who is more important to this company? Those of us who create and make the products or the bosses who do the razzle-dazzle?"

As I listened and probed, I struck emotional chords again and again. A successful corporate banker thanked me profusely for taking time to talk about something important to him. "I've let dozens of researchers and consultants interview me over the years. They've asked about my work, the corporate culture, my views on the firm's strategy, ad nauseam. This is the first time I've talked about something hidden in my heart. Followership speaks to me because it's who I am. I've always been a solid contributor, but others made me feel like that wasn't enough. They always told me to take on more leadership. I never saw the value in it."

Followers at their best, I learned, participate with

enthusiasm, intelligence, and self-reliance—but without star billing—in the pursuit of organizational goals. Far from the stereotype of passive sheep, they are linked together by their individual decisions to make a personal dream or a common dream become a reality.

These followers have the courage to be honest with themselves. In the face of tremendous societal pressure to buy into the leadership myth, they conquer their conformist tendency. Instead, they forge an individual path of followership. They sacrifice societal rewards, like status, money, and fame, to be true to themselves and to find their own meaning in life. Not at all passive sheep or "yes people," they are true "rugged individualists" who have enough ego strength to go their own way.

Paradoxically, "their way" is to work with others when appropriate, rather than compete; to get the job done, rather than vie for power or credit; to stand up for what is right, rather than what gets them promoted; to care in the face of apathy; to know when enough is enough.

These observations mapped well my own experiences in following. I remember when one of my closest friends decided to run for judge in Chicago as an independent Democrat against the machine's candidate. His followers believed that he would be a good judge and an antidote to the rampant judicial corruption. There were some problems, however. He had few political connections and fewer funds. As an assistant state's attorney, he stood to lose his job, just for running against the machine. Everyone involved in his race, including me, was going to make enemies.

During the ten months of the campaign, we

worked our tails off in what turned out to be a nasty campaign, dogged and threatened by machine people at every step.

During the entire time, our "leader" never acted superior to us. We were in this race together. It made little difference who did what. Jobs had to get done if we were going to win. Leader-follower distinctions were invisible.

After ten months of hard work, we did the unexpected—we upset the machine. During the victory celebrations, I had no desire to share center stage with my friend. I only felt pride in our accomplishment and hoped for his success as a judge. I also felt a renewed respect for our democratic system's belief in the ordinary citizen. Not only did it allow a bunch of nobodies to play David to the political machine's Goliath; it also showed that the voters do not follow blindly.

As part of my journey into followership, I also discovered that the demarcation between leaders and the led is not as clear as the leadership myth would have us believe. Unfortunately, leadership and followership have been stereotyped to the detriment of both. If followers are thought of positively at all, it is as apprentice leaders. This is the thesis of West Point and most bureaucratic establishments. Before people are allowed a leadership position, they must prove themselves capable of following. Leadership is the reward for good following. Once you pass the grade, you seldom have to suffer followership again.

Cincinnatus, a farmer and general during the Roman Republic, offers an alternative: that followership and leadership exist side by side. In 458 B.C., the Roman army under the consul Minucius was besieged by the

Aequi, an advancing enemy. The government appointed Cincinnatus to relieve Minucius and to lead the army in its time of need. The messenger found Cincinnatus plowing his fields. Told of his command, Cincinnatus assumed the required dress, left his farm, and took charge of the troops. Within fifteen days, the Romans defeated the Aequi and returned to Rome in triumph. Although the government offered Cincinnatus the title of dictator, he went back to his farm and his place as an ordinary citizen, content with being a follower in peacetime.

Like Cincinnatus, all of us both lead and follow. One is not better than the other; we're called up to do both. Like Cincinnatus, most of us follow much more than we lead. Sure, we might lead our department, but we're a follower to our boss. For every committee or task force we chair, we serve as followers or team members on another. *For most of us, followership represents 70 to 90 percent of our working days.*

Now be honest with yourself. When you are in the follower role, do you think of yourself as fitting the negative stereotype? Are you blindly obedient? Do you stop using your intelligence, motivation, and conscience? Do you wait to be told what to do? My guess is that you are every bit the positive, exemplary follower.

How do you feel when the leader assumes you are mindless and treats you accordingly? Or when the leader acts as if she is better than you? What's it like when the leader grabs the full credit and acts as if it were a solo performance? How do you feel about yourself and the leader?

That leaders don't generally know the answers to these questions suggests that their worst failure is knowing almost nothing about how their behavior affects their followers.

These thoughts and feelings about followership took on a personal urgency when I confronted the raising of my children. Did I want them to become leaders or followers, and what kind of leader or follower? How would they even learn to be effective followers? We teach children to sit still and not talk back. But we don't teach them how to discriminate between good and bad leaders or how to be respectful but skeptical of authority. Our children need to learn how to defend themselves against leaders and against peer pressure. If they had stronger follower skills, we would not need so many leaders, let alone worry about a leadership vacuum.

Followership Now!

The current debate raging in leadership circles today is: Who is more important, leaders or managers? One side argues that organizations need innovative visionaries. The other side protests that organizations need people who can bring professional order and control to the enterprise. The mediators say both are needed. Followers, the 80 to 90 percent who actually do the work, don't even get mentioned.

This debate is totally out of touch with the sweep of history and current events. The democratization of Eastern Europe is a celebration of followership. The Berlin Wall fell not by any act of leadership, but by millions of East Germans joining together to say they wouldn't take it anymore. They wanted soap, fresh fruit, the freedom to travel, to vote—most of all to collectively determine their lives rather than have it imposed by "leaders."

Common people—plumbers, barbers, poets, grocery clerks—have made history happen all over Eastern Europe. Lech Walesa was just an electrician with callused hands and little education. The Western media, with deep roots in the leadership myth, needed someone to play the central role. But as any student of Poland's Solidarity movement knows, Walesa was more the spokesperson than the leader. And isn't it curious that the events in Eastern Europe happened without the benefit of the leadership myth or leadership training? In fact, these were victories of common people over those who had all the leadership training and privileges.

If the United States is faltering now, it is because of a failure of followership more than a failure of leadership. The fate of the United States, and particularly U.S. industry, depends on a return to our roots—a belief in the power of the follower, that we are the ones who ultimately make the difference whether it be at home, at work, in our communities, or in our nation.

Bertolt Brecht captured this lesson well in his poem "A Worker Reads History."

Who built the seven gates of Thebes?
The books are filled with names of kings.
Was it kings who hauled the craggy blocks of
    stone?
And Babylon, so many times destroyed,
Who built the city up each time? In which of
    Lima's houses,

That city glittering with gold, lived those who
    built it?
In the evening when the Chinese wall was
    finished
Where did the masons go? Imperial Rome
Is full of arcs of triumph. Who reared them up?
    Over whom
Did the Caesars triumph? Byzantium lives in
    song,
Were all her dwellings palaces? And even in
    Atlantis of the legend
The night the sea rushed in,
The drowning men still bellowed for their slaves.

Young Alexander conquered India.
He alone?
Caesar beat the Gauls.
Was there not even a cook in his army?
Philip of Spain wept as his fleet
Was sunk and destroyed. Were there no other
    tears?
Frederick the Great triumphed in the Seven
    Years' War. Who
Triumphed with him?

Each page a victory,
At whose expense the victory ball?
Every ten years a great man,
Who paid the piper?

So many particulars.
So many questions.

2. The Difference Between

Success and Failure in the

21st Century Organization

Why have we misunderstood and miscast followers, mistakenly assuming that leaders are the only source of power and achievement? How did we come to see followership as the antithesis of leadership rather than followers as collaborators in the effort of organizational work?

It is important to confront these questions so that we can break the grip of these social stereotypes. Only then can we shape work relationships which maximize everyone's productivity and fulfillment. Only then can we build a new definition of followership—one that embraces followers as fully competent and full partners in the organization.

Part of this effort involves exposing the cultural assumptions and shortcomings of leadership and its mythology. But that is only half the struggle. It is just as important to debunk the negative myth of followership.

A Nation of Sheep
Begets a Government of Wolves

When Bertrand de Jouvenal spoke those words, he meant to describe how followers and leaders are locked in a dramatic dance. Indeed, they always have been.

The word "follower" has its etymological roots in Old High German *follaziohan,* which meant to assist, help, succor, or minister to. This parallels the Old High German root of "leader," which meant to undergo, suffer, or endure. In the original meaning, followers helped take care of leaders, though there are few etymological clues as to why leaders suffered or were in need of care. However, the relationship between them appears to be a symbiotic one between equals.

Over time, follower came to mean "to go or be full in number," as in a crowd. If someone, a leader perhaps, was issuing an edict, appearing in a public forum, or traveling a distance, the people in attendance were called followers. This again did not denote any inferior standing so much as an honor. Christ chose his disciples, just as King Arthur chose the knights for his Round Table. In these cases, the follower gained prestige rather than lost it.

Only in the last hundred years or so have the terms "leader" and "follower" taken on their current connotations. Like the "great person" leadership myth which I traced in the previous chapter to the work of Thomas Carlyle, the negative followership myth has its roots in Social Darwinism. "Survival of the fittest" pits contenders against one another like the ancient Greek gods who battled one another. To struggle and compete is natural, good, and right. The winners, by definition, are leaders; the losers are everyone else.

The Darwinistic viewpoint has infused culturally charged values into the terms "follower" and "leader." It also created a false, hierarchical topography, as if only leaders matter while the remaining 90 to 99 percent of the world is inferior and not worth mapping.

For example, Max DePree, the highly respected chairman of Herman Miller, runs a much admired company. In his best-selling book *Leadership Is an Art,* he makes many nontraditional statements. For instance, he suggests that followership and leadership involve intimacy and personal covenants people at work make with each other. Harking back to the original meaning of the word "leader," he believes that "leaders don't inflict pain; they bear pain." Also, leaders need to get out of the followers' way and say "thank you" more. Although DePree raised a few eyebrows, no one has seriously challenged him. As a successful CEO, he can get away with these views.

But what if Herman Miller "followers" had offered

these same pearls of wisdom. Would anyone have taken them seriously? Is it any less true (or false) because it comes from a follower first? Although followers have as much knowledge of the follower-leader relationship, their views are seldom voiced or heard.

In 1985, I offered a new course, "Followership and Leadership," at Carnegie-Mellon University. Given the surge in downsizings and corporate restructurings, I sensed that business would need to change the way it viewed these roles. As management ranks were thinned, the rank and file would have greater impact on the success or failure of companies. Organizations would need more and more exemplary followers. Yet followership skills had traditionally been neglected. So I decided to try to teach these skills to students, knowing that upon graduation they would play the followership role sooner and longer than the leadership role.

To develop the course materials, I contacted the training departments of major corporations, as well as the top business schools. All had leadership courses. Not one had a program that trained people in follower-ship skills. Most responded as if I were crazy to even think of it.

I was sent a performance evaluation form from a multinational telecommunications company which rated the leadership quality of workers on a scale of 0 to 5. The highest score of 5 was given to individuals de-scribed as "naturally assumes leadership in the group." Workers received a 3 if they "lead when directed." Zero, the bottom score, was reserved for people who "follow." Of course, the form contained no category to rate the quality of an employee's followership skills.

I hoped I would find more empathy, or insight, from

others, from professionals in disciplines like history, literature and drama, business, politics, religion, labor unions, philosophy, biology, journalism, psychology. Yet when I asked them to describe what came to mind when they thought about followers, the number of negative descriptions greatly exceeded the positive ones.

"Sheep" was a favorite term: people who are easily led and manipulated. Many recalled the awful spectacle in Guyana when over three hundred followers of Jim Jones committed mass suicide at his urging.

Others focused on "yes people" who do not think for themselves but who willingly and often enthusiastically carry out another's directives. Adolf Eichmann, one of Hitler's top officials, was an extreme example of this category. In her book *Eichmann in Jerusalem,* Hannah Arendt depicts Eichmann not as a sadistic monster but as a yes-man bureaucrat put in charge of exterminating the Jews. His defense, like that of Oliver North of Iran-Contra fame, was that he did not believe it was his place to question his superiors.

My sources had a difficult time dredging up positive role models like Aristotle, Eleanor Roosevelt, or the twelve apostles. When I remarked that talented, respected people actually chose to follow and enjoyed the role, they reacted skeptically as if these few "adult Boy Scouts" were an aberration. When I pointed out that some actually gave up leadership roles because they preferred the work and rewards of following, they wondered if these people were not simply "happy losers" who realized they couldn't make the leadership grade and had resigned themselves to their predicament.

I then sent students in my course into the community of Pittsburgh to find and interview followers respected by their leaders and co-workers. They found leaders who willingly identified followers for interviews. But then the leaders would warn the students not to call the identified followers, of all things, "followers." And if individuals were informed that they were "followers," they bristled. No one seems to mind being identified as a leader, and people don't mind identifying their leader. But even as people talk about their leaders, many are loath to be considered followers.

This bias against following is found not only in business. It is also reinforced in family life. How many children defend themselves against involvement in a troublesome action by saying, "Well, she did it first." And how many adults reflexively answer, "Are you going to be a follower all your life?" How many parents are not proud when told their child assumed the leadership position. On more than one occasion, parents have confided to me that their son or daughter after years of "plodding" finally started exhibiting leadership qualities. Had the child failed to develop the skills, then by default their fate was the followership caste—an unfortunate fate in our society.

In addition to the existence of a strong negative stereotype of followers, there are people who actively enforce it. I call these people the leadership enthusiasts. These people damn or denigrate followers in the mistaken belief that it enhances leadership. It is the sociological equivalent of a negative political campaign. Leadership enthusiasts often feel threatened when told that followers could be strong, independent-minded people who wanted to contribute as equal partners in the enterprise.

An upper-level manager from Digital Equipment

Corporation once exploded at me, "I'll be damned if my subordinates are going to be like that. I've worked too hard and sacrificed too much to get where I am. I'm not going to let them ruin it. When I give the orders, they better do what they are told. When they get to be the boss, then they can think for themselves."

These leadership enthusiasts remind me of the tropical upas tree. To ward off competitors for sustenance, the tree's branches cast a large shadow to keep out the sunlight that other plants need. Its enormous root system likewise sucks up the surrounding moisture. It drops leaves which poison the ground for other plant life. Like the upas tree, leadership enthusiasts have a vested interest in maintaining the status quo of current social stereotypes.

Why the Myths of Followership Satisfy

In our society, the negative stereotype of followership is deeply rooted. It is part of us. Although I showed the leadership enthusiasts solid examples which refuted the stereotype, many dismissed the examples and clung to their stereotypes. To crack its grip, which stifles the positive power of followership, I needed to understand the purpose the stereotype serves in our culture.

As I pondered, I recalled science critic Jeremy Rifkin's observation about Darwin. In his book *Algeny*, Rifkin argues that Darwin did nothing more than superimpose onto nature the social and economic belief system of 19th century England.

39

Darwin dressed up nature with an English personality, ascribed to nature English motivations and drives, and even provided nature with an English marketplace and the English form of government. Like others who preceded him in history, Darwin borrowed from the popular culture the appropriate metaphors and then transposed them to nature, projecting a new cosmology that was remarkably similar in detail to the everyday life he was accustomed to.

Darwin's theory mirrored his society quite well. It not only reflected England's belief in imperialism and material progress; it also came to justify them.

Rifkin's observation triggered a series of thoughts. I wondered how an observer from another planet would view followership and leadership in the United States. How would they make sense of our stereotypes? Would these stereotypes reflect our society's values and also serve society?

The first observation made by such an observer might be the American character of these stereotypes. Different cultures, such as Japan and Germany, define these terms differently. In those countries, followership can be a noble role that brings societal recognition and personal satisfaction.

Although Japan's samurai are now extinct, their tradition of Bushido continues. Bushido served as both a philosophy of life and a code of conduct. In Bushido, being a faithful follower in the service of one's lord was a major expectation. One's social standing was enhanced mainly via good followership. Although giant corporations have replaced the feudal lords, this spirit of

Bushido still exists in Japan. Thus, rather than try to escape the role, Japanese workers give followership their all, yielding enormous competitive advantage to their companies and country.

Next, the observers might notice how the terms reinforce both our "great person" and Social Darwinist legacies inherited from England. These theories create a social architecture that assures competition within species. If you compete successfully, you are labeled a leader and get power, perks, and privileges. Furthermore, your fate as a winner or loser is *your* responsibility, resulting in your receiving credit or blame. Winners are applauded; losers are stigmatized. In this way the lopsided power structure is justified and promoted.

Our anthropologists also would notice that the leadership myth cannot exist without our corresponding followership myth. "Strong" leaders are redundant if followers are strong in their own right. "Inspirational" leaders are unnecessary if followers have their own dreams and can motivate themselves. "Visionaries" become less important if followers can figure out for themselves where, how, and why they are going. Without the dependent follower, the hero sits idly or postures comically on an empty stage.

In reality, followership and leadership are two separate concepts, two separate roles. They are complementary, not competitive, paths to organizational contribution. Neither role corners the market on brains, motivation, talent, or action. Either role can result in an award-winning performance or a flop. The greatest successes require that the people in both roles turn in top-rate performances. We must have great leaders *and* great followers.

The Long Walk Home, a movie about the 1954 bus boycott by blacks in Montgomery, Alabama, drives this point home. Although the Reverend Martin Luther King, Jr., and other preachers organized the boycott, its success required thousands of blacks to decide individually to forgo the convenience of the buses and walk each day to work and then back home again. Poor, underpaid maids, gardeners, mechanics, and factory workers put their health, livelihoods, and safety on the line day after day to defeat segregation. As one maid's daughter complained, "Why should we walk every day when those preachers don't have to? Their feet don't ache 'cuz they all got fancy cars to drive in." Her mother, Odessa, responds that she's not doing it just for them. She does it for her family and the black community.

Initially a follower in the bus boycott, Odessa tells her white boss, Miriam, that she'll have to find another job because the five-mile walk each way is too difficult. This awakens Miriam's social conscience. For a moment, the roles reverse, with Odessa leading Miriam by inspiring her to join the boycott and to car-pool blacks to their jobs. Finally, when an angry mob of white men confront the car-pool operation, Odessa and Miriam lead the nonviolent resistance.

What we cheer in this portrayal is how people can rise to the role of leader or follower. These roles are not personality types. We can simultaneously lead subordinates on a task force and then follow someone else's lead on another committee. Followership and leadership are synergistic more than separate, and interchangeable more than caste-conscious.

Lewis Thomas, the former dean at Yale Medical

School, makes a similar observation about the artificial separatism between people and nature. In his prize-winning book *Lives of a Cell,* he muses:

> Humans are embedded in nature . . . A good case can be made for our nonexistence as entities. We are not made up, as we had always supposed, of successively enriched packets of our own parts. We are shared, rented, occupied. At the interior of our cells, driving them, providing the oxidative energy that sends us out for the improvement of each shining day, are the mitochondria, and in a strict sense they are not ours. They turn out to be separate little creatures . . . with their own DNA and RNA quite different from ours. They are as much symbionts as the rhizobial bacteria in the roots of beans. Without them, we would not move a muscle, drum a finger, think a thought.
>
> I like to think that they work in my interest, that each breath they draw for me, but perhaps it is they who walk through the local park in the early morning, sensing my sense, listening to my music, thinking my thoughts.
>
> Most of the association between the living things we know are essentially cooperative ones, symbiotic in one degree or another; when they have the look of adversaries, it is usually a standoff relationship, with one party issuing signals, warnings, flagging the other off . . . we do not have solitary beings. Every creature is, in some sense, connected to and dependent on the rest.

If we take off our Darwinistic blinders, we see this truth all around us. Sharks are viewed as "leaders" in the sea world. Frequently smaller fish swim alongside them. The casual watcher sees these fish as parasites who feed off remnants of the shark's kills and which are protected by being in the "leader's" shadow. In this view, the shark provides but gets nothing in return.

The reality is much more complex and symbiotic. Some "cleaner" fish actually eat the parasites that attach themselves to the shark's skin. Without the cleaner fish, the shark's life would be endangered. So who is protecting whom?

Other fish, I've discovered, like the pointer fish, identify the shark's food. Like the lion, which actually depends on hyenas to find and kill the prey for many of its meals, the shark depends on these pointer fish to pinpoint dinner.

But these comparisons from nature don't quite capture the interdependence, and often the indistinguishability, of human followers and leaders. I remember when I played guard on a football team. Most football fans believe that the quarterback is the team's leader on the field and that the rest of us do what we're told. The reality is quite different.

During one season, a new quarterback believed he was the team leader. In the season opener, he ranted about how we weren't doing anything, that he was the only one really performing. Those of us on the line, whose job it was to protect him during play, decided to let him know what we were really doing. We let the other team crush him two or three times in a row. In the huddle, we let him know that he needed us more than we needed him. If he felt that he was better than the rest of us, then he was in for a long season.

Likewise, Ronald Reagan is commonly perceived

as an important leader in recent American history. According to the mythmakers, he restored the United States to its rightful place as the world's leader, turned around the economy via "Reaganomics," and caused the conservative swing in American society.

Yet I have heard it alternately argued that Reagan was not the true leader at all. He was simply the front for a group of people who aspired to power, including Ed Meese, Michael Deaver, and Nancy Reagan. Over a twenty-year period they shaped, molded, and used him, taking advantage of his acting skills and popularity. According to this interpretation, Reagan was the follower who played his greatest part by mouthing words given to him by others. He allowed the budget deficit to bankrupt the country, the S&L mess to undermine our banking system, and corrupt HUD officials to enrich themselves at the expense of the homeless—not because he was turning a blind eye as leader, but because he wasn't really in charge.

So the question arises: What are the qualities of the leader and what are those of the follower, especially when those qualities are found in one and same person?

Followership and leadership are a dialectic. Just as the word "right" makes no sense without "left," they depend upon each other for existence and meaning. They can never be independent. But unlike right and left, it is not always so easy to sort out who is leading and who is following. As Lewis Thomas asks, who's in charge of our bodies? Do I eat because I choose to or am I commanded to eat by the bacteria in my intestines who want food and without whom I would die? Do the sharks command the smaller fish or are they led by them? Was my quarterback the leader or was the leadership held by those of us who disciplined him?

We Need Exemplary Followers

Some people argue that we may need a new vocabulary to describe followership and leadership if we are to overcome our cultural blinders. But I am not hopeful that it will happen.

No one wants to give up the word "leadership." We have too much of our identity wrapped up in it to discard it. When I suggested to audiences that I would gladly stop using the term "followership" if we delete "leadership" from our vocabulary, people responded with shock, as if I were suggesting we deface the Statue of Liberty. It is a cultural beacon without which we fear we cannot find our way in the darkness.

But if we insist on using the term "leadership," don't we have to keep "followership"? When you cut through all the platitudes defining leadership, doesn't it boil down to this: *that the leader is someone who can attract and retain followers?* Without followers, leadership is meaningless and leaders don't exist. Synonyms for followers—associates, colleagues, co-adventurers, fellows, companions, corporate citizens, members, team players—do not capture how leaders and followers are bound to each other. As you can't have a husband without a wife, a daughter without parents, or a teacher without students, leaders and followers need each other to exist and have meaning.

A more important reason for keeping the term "followership" is that our society does value followers, albeit in limited ways. Would Columbus have made it to the New World if three hundred sailors were not willing to follow him? America would not be what it is today if boatload after boatload had not followed in the *Mayflower*'s wake. The Revolutionary War would have been no more than a tavern "putsch" if the followers had not made it happen. Women still would not vote had not American citizens followed Susan B. Anthony. The environmental movement is fueled by followers who want to head off the global catastrophe depicted in Rachel Carson's book *Silent Spring*.

Our social fabric depends on followership; without it, society unravels. The family structure needs children to follow parents, as our democracy ceases if citizens do not follow the leaders they elect.

So the question is not *whether* to have followers, but what *kind* of followers we want. I think what we want is "good" followership—people who take appropriate actions with great skill and achievement. We don't want the mindless subordinates who need vast attention. Rather than let effective followers be devalued by the tarnish heaped on the stereotype of followers, shouldn't we begin to differentiate between them?

We may have little choice but to make these distinctions vivid. A confluence of historical and sociological events demands that we produce strong exemplary followers. Yet this cannot happen until we legitimate and appreciate the inherent value and dignity in following. From global democratization to corporate downsizing, our society is becoming increasingly dependent on followers for success. We need people who are not only willing but also capable of playing the role well.

We need people like Thomas Jefferson, who assumed the followership role on several occasions during the Revolutionary War. Most people think of Jefferson's writing of the Declaration of Independence as a leadership feat. But in reality Jefferson was a follower when he wrote it. As the "junior" member of the committee, he was assigned the task by the committee chairs, John Adams and Ben Franklin. Nobody outside of the Continental Congress, except a few friends, knew that Jefferson had written the Declaration. The fact did not appear in an American newspaper until eight years later in 1784. As a follower, Jefferson lived through all the bell ringing and speechmaking with little public recognition or personal commendation in the press.

The Declaration of Independence is just one example of the great results that motivated followers can produce. Followers who understand the value of their role and learn to live fully in it can accomplish great organizational and personal triumphs—sometimes well beyond what a leader, circumscribed by power and dependencies on followers, can ever quite achieve.

3. Why Become

a Follower?

Why would anyone of perseverance, spirit, and intelligence slow a career before reaching the top or choose not to strive for it in the first place? How did Aristotle choose to follow Plato? How did Carl Jung find his way to Sigmund Freud?

What led Ellen Gates Starr to follow Jane Addams and make Hull-House an international achievement in providing a settlement center for Chicago's poor immigrants.

Understanding why people follow is important to leaders and followers alike. Knowing these motivations, one can design organizational environments to attract, accommodate, and retain followers. If leaders understand followers' motivations, they can better respond to them and avoid the risk of losing their followers.

A misunderstanding of motivations can create disasters of even good intentions. For example, too many leaders believe that people follow a leader's charisma or vision. Thus, leaders will often expend great effort in trying to become charismatic or to shape a vision. In reality, only some followers look for these characteristics. Others are motivated by their own personal vision that they want to bring to life. Many are wary of charisma. Instead, they prefer leaders as co-adventurers who facilitate achieving a goal.

Why do people decide against the leadership role? It occurs when they discover these appealing paths of followership:

- Apprentice
- Disciple
- Mentee
- Comrade
- Loyalist
- Dreamer
- Lifeway

Each of these paths is characterized by different sets of motivations.*

The first six paths are discussed in this chapter. The last path—lifeway—is discussed in the next chapter.

FIGURE 1.
Seven Paths to Followership

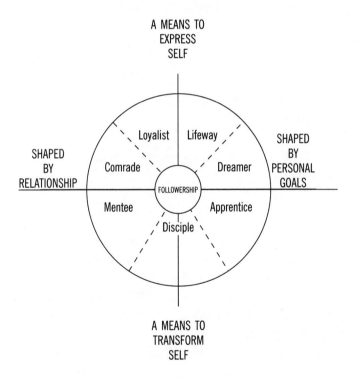

* Although other followership paths exist, either they are not as well used as these paths or they are an offshoot of one path. For example, I do not discuss cultism because it derives from discipleship.

Expressing Oneself versus Transforming Oneself

Some of these paths serve as a vehicle for expressing oneself. Individuals who choose this course are generally comfortable with their talents, lifestyle, and personal accomplishments. They are motivated by a desire to contribute their skills toward organizational goals.

Other paths serve as a means of transforming oneself. These people are not satisfied with who they are. They seek personal growth in order to become a different and better person.

For example, G. I. Gurdjieff, the Russian philosopher and teacher, kept himself in an unformed state so that he could continually transform himself. In his book *Meetings with Remarkable Men,* he recounts how he traveled throughout Asia and Europe in search of teachers from whom he could learn. He saw this continual rebirth as an essential task of living, rather than a one-time event.

Relationship Bonding versus Personal Goals

Some followers appreciate the interpersonal involvement of followership. People who value these bonds follow people more than goals or dreams.

Others have an intrapersonal focus. They see followership, not primarily as a relationship with others, but a vehicle for achieving personal dreams. Many of the early NASA engineers worked together for ten years to put a person on the moon. But the goal, not their relationship, motivated them to follow.

These distinctions are not absolute or mutually exclusive. Each of us is likely to follow one or more of these followership paths during our lives. Or we may also travel down some of them simultaneously. A closer look at each is in order.

Apprentice

Perhaps the most easily identified followership path is the one chosen by those "aspiring to be" leaders. They understand the need to learn the ropes and pay their dues. By proving themselves in the follower's role, they hope to win the confidence of peers and superiors. They accept the value of doing a good job in the role, studying leadership from the followers' perspective, and polishing followership skills, like teamwork and self-management, that will always stand them in good stead. Many women residents of Jane Addams's Hull-House, for example, saw it as "a training ground for new professional careers as experts and administrators in government, industry, and the universities."

Comedian Phil Silvers once said, "If you wanna be top banana, you gotta start at the bottom of the bunch." This sentiment harks all the way back to Aristotle. In his *Politics,* he observed that Greece's would-be leaders, like many graduating MBAs today, wanted to start at the top and *then* work their way up. Decrying their power lust, Aristotle insisted that training as a nonleader was a necessary part of growing to leadership.

Who would learn to lead must . . . first of all learn to obey. Some things differ not in the thing commanded, but in the intention with which they are imposed. That is why many apparently menial offices are an honor to the free by whom they are performed; for actions do not differ as honorable or dishonorable in themselves so much as in the end and intention of them. But since we say that the excellence of the citizen and the ruler is the same as that of the good person, and that the same person must first be a subject and then a ruler, the rulers must first become good people.

The philosopher Hegel echoes Aristotle by requiring followership as a precondition of leadership. In *Phenomenology of Mind,* Hegel proposes the "dialectic of master and slave." According to Hegel, the best masters are those who have known servitude. The act of personally passing through followership sears the followership experience into the leader's psyche.

Most armies have made faithful service in the ranks a prerequisite for advancement. William Litzinger and Thomas Schaefer, two business professors from the University of Texas System, discovered the apprenticeship phenomenon in their work with the U.S. Army. They posed the following question to a group of officers, most of whom were on the West Point faculty and many of whom were themselves graduates of the Academy. "Since developing leadership is what this place is all about," they asked, "how do you go about doing that task?" The officers' answer surprised the researchers. "We begin by teaching them to be followers."

From this, Litzinger and Schaefer formulated their West Point Thesis—"the mastery of followership may prepare and qualify one for leadership." By this they mean that officers must spend time in the ranks, learning what it is like to be directed and commanded. They must learn the rules and be subjected to them before they are allowed to issue their own orders. Finally, would-be leaders must master the skills necessary for leadership. Once they master lower-level skills, they are allowed to lead in situations suited for those skills, while they remain a follower in all other aspects. From their vantage point, some of the best leaders in history began as excellent followers. In his youth, Churchill distinguished himself as an able subordinate. Otto von Bismark did the same, working his way up through the German bureaucracy.

In fact, followership as apprenticeship is the method of choice in most large bureaucracies. China's "mandarin court" system provides an early example. When the Han dynasty unified China around 200 B.C., it faced the enormous task of administering this far-flung, most populous country on earth. Rather than resort to nepotism, which had always led to degeneration, the Han rulers innovated the mandarin system. The precursor to our modern civil service system, it chose administrators on the basis of their knowledge of and obedience to Confucian principles, which constituted a code both for personal living and for how to govern.

The Hans desired to place the best people in government, regardless of family background or social standing, and to always infuse new blood into the system. A high-ranking official's child received no preference over a peasant. A national test was open to all.

Once candidates entered the mandarinate, their ascent to leadership depended upon their performance in lower ranks. At each level, their service was evaluated on the basis of Confucian principles. Mastery prepared them for their next promotion.

China's mandarin system influenced other bureaucracies, ranging from the British civil service system to the Catholic Church. As Edward Page, a British political scientist, noted in his book *Political Authority and Bureaucratic Power:* "In Britain . . . eligibility for promotions to the higher levels of service of Under Secretary, Deputy Secretary and Permanent Secretary is contingent on the performance in the more junior ranks up to Assistant Secretary. Both promotion within the lower ranks and promotion from lower to the higher levels . . . results from a successful interview with a promotion board composed of civil servants." Note that this is basically a peer-review system. Promotion requires both performing well as a follower and satisfying those whom you will lead.

Japanese businesses also require long apprenticeships and socialization periods. In comparison, their American counterparts often scale the corporate ladder quickly but superficially. After six months or a year, American managers move on to new jobs, whether or not they have mastered their current responsibilities.

Japanese executives, on the other hand, will spend several years at each rung. This allows them to master every detail, nuance, and contingency of each level. When they face a stressful situation, this training and mastery gives them an intimate and seemingly intuitive understanding of its impact at all the different levels through which they have passed. They also have a wide and complex repertoire of ingrained responses to fall back on, unlike the more shallow set of their fast-track U.S. counterparts.

Disciple

Discipleship is seldom discussed in today's secular world. Relegated to religion, discipleship conjures up images of crowds gathered at a master's feet, hanging on every word. Yet some truly remarkable followers began as disciples.

For example, having read Plato's dialogues, the seventeen-year-old Aristotle left his hometown for Athens to study in Plato's Academy. By all accounts, this was the crucial event in Aristotle's development as a philosopher and scientist. He even referred to this event in his writing. According to Jonathan Barnes, an Aristotelian scholar, "In one of his lost works, Aristotle told how a Corinthian farmer had happened to read Plato's *Gorgias* and 'at once gave up his farm and his vines, mortgaged his soul to Plato, and sowed and planted it with Plato's philosophy.' " For the next twenty formative years, Aristotle worked and studied with a brilliant group of disciples under Plato's leadership. Had Plato not died, he would have stayed longer under Plato's tutelage.

The word "disciple" comes from the Greek. Its original meaning was "one who is learning from a teacher." Traditionally, disciples like Aristotle put themselves under the guidance of one who was more learned. Disciples would live with their teacher, share meals, and converse frequently. Unlike mentorship, which is an intensive one-on-one experience aimed at personal maturation, discipleship involves a body of knowledge being passed from a teacher to a group of students. Generally, it involved intellectual, not emotional development.

This original form of discipleship consisted of education, not indoctrination in any set of beliefs. Plato was no polymath, according to Barnes, nor did he pretend to the range of disciplines which his most famous disciple mastered. Although Plato focused primarily on philosophy, he did not demand that his students limit themselves. Instead, he encouraged his disciples to research other subjects, which, in turn, attracted the best minds in Greece to his Academy.

Likewise, Plato did not demand strict adherence to his views. Aristotle, who praised Plato as a man "whom it is not right for evil men to even praise," was no card-carrying Platonist. Although Aristotle clearly loved and was greatly influenced by Plato, he felt free to criticize him. Plato even nicknamed Aristotle the Foal. Why? Because foals kick their mothers when they have had enough milk. Some ancient critics accused the disciple of ingratitude, but Plato knew better. A good teacher does not require adherence as a show of gratitude.

As time went on, discipleship took on another dimension. It moved beyond learning to mean "one who believes." It implies an act of conversion to a certain viewpoint. This conversion moves beyond intellectual judgment to an emotional commitment and obedience. It also leads to witnessing—that is, spreading to others what you have learned.

We generally place this form of discipleship in the context of religion. St. Mark's gospel in the New Testament describes how Levi became a disciple of Jesus. "And as [Jesus] passed by he saw Levi, the son of Alphaeus, sitting at the place of toll, and he saith unto him, Follow me. And he arose and followed him."

Dietrich Bonhöffer, the German theologian who was executed for participating in the plot on Hitler's life, addressed this new definition of discipleship in his book *The Cost of Discipleship*. For him, discipleship has two elements: faith and obedience. With these two acts, you forsake your previous existence for the promise of a new life. Simultaneously, you break your old ties and adhere exclusively to the new. For the religious, this act of discipleship is the first step on the road to salvation.

The psychology behind this form of followership is identification. Followers want to bond with and emulate the leader. They are willing to become a part of something that is bigger, better, or more important than they are individually. Unlike mentorship, where followers hope to develop into the person they want to be, disciples give up a current persona to take on a new one— one that makes the followers seem to enlarge themselves.

This form of discipleship, however, is not exclusive to religion. When Sigmund Freud published his *Interpretation of Dreams* in 1900, he was a lone voice on the fringe of established medical science. Although he launched psychoanalysis, he did not change the course of psychology single-handedly. His help came from disciples who gathered around him.

In 1902, Freud invited four physicians to discuss psychoanalysis on Wednesday evenings. By 1906, the group called itself the Psychological Wednesday Society and included seventeen members. At its inception, it resembled Plato's Academy more than a religion. Members would share their pioneering research and writing with others for both criticism and support. Freud refrained from pontificating; rather he facilitated the group's thinking and harmony.

As time progressed, however, education gave way

to orthodoxy. The new members who joined the group were no longer just explorers; they were believers. When Carl Jung first visited Freud in 1907, he came as a believer ready to carry the Freudian banner. Irving Stone recounts their meeting in *The Passions of the Mind:*

> Carl Jung . . . paced the room, fitting long strides to the sentences happily tumbling out of him . . . "Highly Revered Professor, I have looked forward to this moment for years. Without your work I would never have had a key to my own work . . . you have lighted up the sky with the new sun of the unconscious. Before you began to explore the unconscious we lived in a dark cave as far as understanding human motivation or character was concerned. It's the difference between our ancestors who lived in the forests with clubs as their only means of procuring food, and those who came out into the bright light to plant and till the fields."
>
> The gratifying part of the morning was that Carl Jung appeared to be holding nothing back. With every gesture . . . every relevant sentence . . . was an avowal that he was a Freudian; that he intended to stand shoulder to shoulder with the older man; to teach the meaning and measure of the unconscious mind to a disinterested world. Jung was exulting in the fact that Sigmund Freud was his teacher, guide, inspiration; he made it clear in every ringing sentence that "I am a disciple of Sigmund Freud."

With Freud's growing insistence and Jung's help, psychoanalysis became an orthodoxy. It was no longer enough to learn; one now had to believe.

This same drama was played out in other modern-day discipleships. In *Judgment Day: My Years with Ayn Rand,* Nathaniel Branden describes how Ayn Rand's Objectivist movement began and flourished. Branden, who became Rand's intellectual heir and lover, relates how disciples formed around her. Known as the Collective, they included Branden, Alan Greenspan (who became chair of the Federal Reserve Board), and several others—all of whom were twenty years Rand's juniors. These people flocked to her because of the power of her ideas. Branden recounts her effect on him.

> I was seeing myself . . . reading *The Fountainhead* for the first time. I was recalling the sense of a door opening, intellectually, spiritually, psychologically—a passageway into another dimension, like a summons from the future.
>
> I read and reread *The Fountainhead* almost continuously, with the dedication and passion of a student of the *Talmud* . . . When I opened its pages, I was transported into a world where the issues I cared about really mattered.

After meeting Rand, Branden became her first and most important disciple. Together, they spearheaded the Collective and launched the Objectivist movement (which also gave rise to the Libertarian Party). After one of their many get-togethers, Branden wrote:

> At such moments as this, my feeling of family was strongest. I felt: here is my home; here is my space; here are my roots. I was conscious of my longing for a sense of roots and I welcomed it . . . I felt as if I had broken free of gravity, as if I dwelt in an unobstructed universe where anything was possi-

ble, as if all obstacles could be overcome, all problems could be solved, and no pain need be taken too seriously.

Although seldom labeled as such, discipleship permeates many fields. The disciples of Keynesian economics fight with Milton Friedman's free-market disciples. Psychological behaviorists challenge the Freudians. Mathematically minded philosophers cannot understand why European philosophers still reason with words rather than numbers.

Organizations and leaders need to pay attention to people who follow as disciples. They can serve as valuable conduits of organizational culture and knowledge. They can represent the leader as missionaries who carry the message to others.

Mentee

Abraham Zaleznik, a Harvard Business School professor, brought the age-old practice of mentoring into the current limelight with his seminal writings on the topic. Mentoring is different from apprenticing in its intensive one-on-one relationship between mentor and follower, which enables the follower to mature.

As Zaleznik noted, "people with great talents are often indifferent students." Dwight Eisenhower's mediocre record in high school and West Point did not foreshadow his later achievements. The reason for his mediocrity obviously was not a lack of ability. Instead, to overcome mediocrity, he needed to form a deep attachment to someone who could help him cultivate his talent.

Zaleznik traced how a mentoring experience transformed Eisenhower's career from competent to outstanding. During World War I, Eisenhower found himself dead-ended "in the monotony and unsought safety of the Zone of the Interior . . . an intolerable punishment," while his classmates were fighting and getting promoted in France.

After World War I, Zaleznik notes, Eisenhower asked for a transfer to Panama to work under General Fox Connor, a senior officer whom he admired. The Army refused the request. This setback further diminished Eisenhower's expectations about his career chances. Shortly thereafter, his firstborn son, Ikey, died from influenza. Without explanation the Army quickly reversed itself and transferred Eisenhower to Panama under Connor's command.

The two men immediately formed a bond, almost like that between father and son. Connor helped Eisenhower reintegrate a life shattered by disappointment and grief. As Eisenhower wrote later, "Life with General Connor was sort of a graduate school in military affairs and the humanities, leavened by a man who was experienced in his knowledge of men and their conduct. I can never adequately express my gratitude to this one gentleman . . . In a lifetime of association with great and good men, he is the one more or less invisible figure to whom I own an incalculable debt."

After his followership experience with General Connor, Eisenhower received a coveted appointment to the Army's Command and General Staff School at Fort Leavenworth. Unlike his West Point performance, Eisenhower met the challenge of this highly competitive school and changed his career trajectory. He graduated first in his class.

Followers like Eisenhower entrust themselves, emotionally and developmentally, to someone who perceives their talents as perhaps a "diamond in the rough." The mentor helps shape the diamond so that it sparkles. The mentor in this case often directs the mentee's talents toward goals where she or he can achieve great satisfaction.

The psychological readiness of an individual to benefit from this form of followership depends upon the individual's ability to "surrender" to the mentor's influence. Often, some experience in life—the death of a loved one, getting fired from a job—triggers this readiness, this dependence on another.

Whereas the goal of apprenticeship is mastery of skills, the goal of mentoring is personal maturation. People who follow a mentor do so for personal benefit. But the followers who seek out mentors are not always trying to become leaders. They may simply see the mentoring relationship as a way of bettering themselves.

In his award-winning play *Fences,* August Wilson depicts the relationship between two black garbage collectors, Troy and Bono. As Wilson notes in the stage directions, "Of the two men, Bono is obviously the follower. His commitment to their friendship of thirty-odd years is rooted in his admiration of Troy's honesty, capacity for hard work, and his strength, which Bono seeks to emulate."

In the play Bono reveals to Troy why he chose to follow him:

Troy . . . I done known you seem like damn near my whole life. You and Rose both. I done know both of you all for a long time. I remember when you met Rose. When you was hitting them baseball out the park. A lot of them old gals was after you then. You had the pick of the litter. When you picked Rose, I was happy for you. That was the first time I knew you had any sense. I said . . . My man Troy knows what he's doing . . . I'm gonna follow this nigger . . . he might take me somewhere. I been following you too. I done learned a whole heap of things about life watching you. I done learned how to tell where the shit lies. How to tell it from the alfalfa. You done learned me a lot of things. You showed me how to not make the same mistakes . . . to take life as it comes along and keep putting one foot in front of the other.
(Pause)
Rose a good woman, Troy.

Bono and followers like him hope to be better people, which will then allow them to be better contributors. Charlotte, a successful administrator at the University of Texas, likewise sought out a mentoring relationship. "From my very first job, I always looked to work for somebody whom I thought I could learn from. I work best when I've got somebody above me whom I can trust. I want someone who will take me in and show me the ropes, someone who is secure enough to let me get close. I'm talking about people who see part of their job as helping me develop.

"I've actually turned down promotions because I didn't feel that I would learn from the new person I would report to. When I'm learning, I'm growing. That's important to me. I look for leaders who will stretch me. I look for those talented, gifted people who have something more to offer me than a job title and some perks."

Like apprentices, mentees choose to be followers to help transform themselves. Whereas apprentices learn to master certain skills, however, mentees seek personal maturation.

Organizations need to link up mentees with suitable mentors. These mentors must have the interpersonal skills, the technical mastery, and the desire to give of themselves so that others can grow. When they work successfully, mentoring relationships produce valuable assets for the organization. When they fail, the organization can lose both parties' future contributions.

Comrade

There are moments in the life of following when being part of a community shapes your followership. Your reason for following may have nothing to do with getting ahead, personal growth, or intellectual development. Instead, it may be about the intimacy and social support that develop when people bond together.

Comradeship is found in any endeavor that requires the effort and talents of more than one person, such as sports teams, orchestras, or building a supercomputer. People also band together as a way of coping with stress. Study groups that help each member get through the first year of law school create a bond that continues long after graduation. Medical interns who survive internship together feel a tremendous closeness to each other. In these situations, you follow for mutually reinforcing reasons: your feeling of goodwill toward the group and the belief that survival is more likely if you collectively share and watch out for each other.

William Broyles, Jr., a former editor in chief of *Newsweek* who served in Vietnam as a Marine lieutenant, described how comradeship emerged during the war. In *Brothers in Arms,* he relates his return to Vietnam ten years later to meet his former enemies.

> I am a peace-loving man, fond of children and animals. In high school I was in the history club instead of on the football team. I believe passionately that war should have no place in the affairs of men, and that the existence of nuclear arsenals means that the emotions that lead to wars can no longer be indulged . . . But a part of me loved war, and at Duy Xuyen I discovered my old enemies felt the same way . . .
>
> We loved war for many reasons, not all of them good. The best reason we loved war is also its most enduring memory—comradeship. A comrade in war is a man you can trust with anything, because you trust him with your life. Philip Caputo described the emotion in *A Rumor of War:* "[Comradeship] does not demand for its sustenance the reciprocity, the pledges of affection, the endless reassurances required by the love of men and women. It is, unlike marriage, a bond that cannot be broken by a word, by boredom or divorce, or by anything other than death."
>
> Comradeship isn't a particularly selective pro-

cess. Race, personality, education—anything that would make a difference in peace—count for nothing. It is, simply, brotherly love. War is the only utopian experience most of us ever have. Individual possessions and advantage count for nothing; the group is everything. What you have is shared with your friends. No one is allowed to be alone.

And in war loneliness is the greatest enemy. The military historian S. L. A. Marshall did intensive studies of combat incidents in World War II and Korea and discovered that at most only 25 percent of the men under fire actually fired their weapons. The rest cowered behind cover, terrified and helpless—all systems off. Invariably, those men had felt alone, and to feel alone in combat is to cease to function; it is the terrifying prelude to the final loneliness of death. The men who kept their heads felt connected to other men, a part of something, as if comradeship were a collective life force, the power to face death and stay conscious.

Yet comradeship is not forged only during stressful times. Sometimes it happens when people are working together for a good cause. For example, Jane Addams, Julia Lathrop, and Florence Kelley formed the inner circle of Hull-House during the early years. Unlike the disciples and apprentices who gathered around Addams, Lathrop and Kelley were comrades-in-arms. They addressed each other in their letters as "Dear Sister" and developed a sense of camaraderie, of dedication to an ideal that was based on respect, commitment, and love.

While in graduate school at the University of Texas, I was lucky enough to land a job at the university's budding Career Choice and Information Center. Bob Murff, the director, had a bold new concept. Rather than creating a traditional center where students simply took a vocational test and met with a counselor, he wanted to build a center that empowered the students. It would have a library where students could research different jobs, companies, and industries. We would offer seminars on how to research job alternatives, explore your own work values, make decisions, and get jobs. The staff would help students take charge of their lives.

Bob gathered around him a staff that could make this happen. Together, we transformed the way career counseling was done at the university. In the process, we became like a family. We helped each other out in times of need—whether on the job or off. We worked nights and weekends to meet deadlines. We were in it for each other and the goal. No one was jockeying to get ahead.

Freeman Dyson, the award-winning physicist at Princeton, had a similar experience when he began his scientific apprenticeship at Cornell. Arriving shortly after World War II, he was surprised to find in residence a large fraction of the Los Alamos group that had built the atom bomb. Han Bethe, his boss, had found jobs for as many as possible of the bright young people at Los Alamos. In *Disturbing the Universe,* Dyson relates:

There was endless talk about the Los Alamos days. Through all the talk shone a glow of pride and nostalgia. For every one of these people, the Los Alamos days had been a great experience, a time of hard work and comradeship and deep happiness. I had the impression that the main reason they were happy to be at Cornell was that the Cornell physics department still retained something of the Los Alamos atmosphere. I, too, could feel the vivid presence of this atmosphere. It was youth, it was exuberance, it was informality, it was a shared ambition to do great things together in science without any personal jealousies or squabbles over credit. Han Bethe and Dick Feynman did, many years later, receive well-earned Nobel Prizes, but nobody at Cornell was grabbing for prizes or for personal glory.

The psychology behind comradeship is one of intimacy that comes from belonging. When Pat Riley was the coach of the very successful Los Angeles Lakers, he was asked, "Why do your players work so hard?" He replied, "The game is about the primal instinct to be part of something." Once you feel part of something you transcend your feelings of isolation and even your feelings of self. This explains why people follow rather than seek personal glory, and why they give their all so that their comrades can succeed.

Organizations and leaders like Pat Riley can utilize this desire to belong to further the organization's goals. Followers with this kind of motivation make great team players. They should be assigned to projects where team cohesion and morale make a difference. For example, projects with tight deadlines, SWAT teams that handle crises, or teams that go head to head with competitors are excellent vehicles for these followers. On the other hand, they may be less comfortable when they are given lengthy solo assignments or expected to compete as an individual against other individuals.

Loyalist

Some people follow out of personal loyalty to the leader. Leonard Peikoff, the protector of Ayn Rand's philosophy after she and Nathaniel Branden parted ways, proudly described himself as the "feudal serf" of Ayn Rand's cause.

For some, this loyalty is an inherent obligation of existence. Fierce loyalty was expected of Japan's samurai. At the center of the code of Bushido, loyalty is of paramount importance and is its distinctive feature. Unlike the Chinese system, in which Confucian ethics made obedience to parents the primary human duty, Japanese Bushido gave precedence to loyalty to the leader.

In *Shogun,* James Clavell depicts the fierce loyalty demanded by Bushido. Hiro-matsu, the commander in chief of Lord Toranaga's army, begins to question his lord's decision to surrender. But rather than depose Toranaga and lead the soldiers in battle, he acts according to Bushido. Like the loyal follower he is, he discusses his concern with his lord:

> "By all gods I only wish to be your most devoted vassal. I'm only a soldier. I wish to do my duty to you. I think only of you. I merit your trust. If it will help, take my head. If it will convince you to fight, I gladly give you my life, my clan's lifeblood, today— in public or private or whatever you wish."

For other leaders, followers' loyalty is hard-earned. In *The Last Hurrah,* Edwin O'Connor describes how

John Gorman, the most powerful ward boss in Boston, earned the loyalty of his followers.

> It was he who found jobs and homes for the recently arrived, who supplied funds in time of distress, who arranged for hospitalization and the payment of medical bills, who gave the son of the family his start in life and the subsequent necessary pushes up the ladder, who built the playgrounds for the children of this populous district, and who, in these days when the aged, the helpless, and the indigent had come to depend increasingly upon government beneficence, saw to it that the baffling complexity of preliminary paper work was solved and that funds were ultimately secured. He had won for his efforts the devotion and obedience of most who lived within the ward, and this in turn, as it was the largest ward in the city, had given him an extraordinary political significance.

It is not unusual for political appointees to follow their leaders in and out of office. Nor is it unusual for key subordinates to follow their bosses up the organizational ladder or from one company to the next. As one of these corporate loyalists confided in me, "I can't imagine working for anyone else. I believe in her. I trust her judgment. We can communicate almost telepathically. Plus, I've done very well. Every time I help her advance, I'm also helping myself."

The basis of some loyalties is difficult to identify. Consider Sancho Panza, the squire of Don Quixote. For years, he followed his hallucinating master, who unwittingly jousts with windmills thinking them monsters.

Time and again he rescued Quixote from misfortune. When Quixote falls in love with Aldonza, the village whore, it is loyal Sancho who must explain the situation to her. She knows Quixote is crazy, but thinks Sancho must be even crazier for following him. When she presses him as to why he follows Quixote, he stammers. He can't put his finger on it. Finally, he blurts out, "I like him."

The followership path of loyalty, like that of comradeship, results from an emotional commitment to another. Deep within, you choose to follow this leader. You give your word. Unlike comradeship, it is one to one— follower to leader. Unlike the personal relationship of mentoring, it has little to do with personal maturation. Instead, it is commitment, willingly given and unshakable from the outside. Only the two people can tear it asunder.

Organizations and leaders who garner such loyalty are fortunate. Having followers who go to extraordinary lengths to serve your interests is a tremendous asset that will be reflected on the bottom line. Moreover, these followers can be entrusted with assignments in which confidentiality and steadfastness are essential. They also can be a valuable conduit for information about lower levels of the organization which may be inaccessible to the leader.

For their part, organizations and leaders must not betray the trust bestowed upon them. This means keeping the follower informed and not intentionally doing things that cause the follower to question the return of loyalty.

Dreamer

Many of the best followers, however, are committed to their personal dream rather than to a particular leader. They are so focused on achieving their dream that it does not matter whether they are in the leader or follower role.

One staffer with a local diabetes society put it this way.

> My mother led a restricted life and died early because of this dreadful condition. I work at this every day in hopes of saving another family from the pain we experienced. My goal is to eradicate it, like smallpox. I feel fortunate that I can get paid to carry out my life's ambition. If not, I'd still do what I could in my free time. I don't have career ambitions per se; I just want to do whatever it takes, whether fund raising or cleaning test tubes or giving workshops to families. Our executive director is very capable and is doing a great job. Sure, I think I could do her job. But that's not the point. We're in this together, trying to make the dream come true.

These people may follow a leader not because of who the leader is but because the leader embodies the idea or the cause. David Newell, a longtime follower of Fred Rogers, the creator of the children's television program *Mister Rogers' Neighborhood,* summarized the reason that he and others there follow.

Most people think we're in the TV business. But we're not. We're in the child development business. Our goal is to help children and families grow. Everything we do has the message at its core. That's what has kept me here for so long. And Fred believes in it most of all. I love and admire Fred. He is rightfully the leader here. But his greatest talent is not his leadership or music or puppetry or his gentleness or even his ability to relate to kids. It's his emphasis on the values. If Fred or this organization ever moved away from these, then that's when I'd probably leave.

This follower is interested in the message first and the leader second.

The dream is the guiding force. During adolescence, Nathaniel Branden confided to his sister, "What I would like to find, someday, is a great issue, a battle, a crusade . . . something really worth fighting for . . . something that would require and demand everything I am and everything I've got to give . . . something important." After reading Ayn Rand's *The Fountainhead*, Branden found a battle that was worth fighting.

Echoing Branden's longing, William Broyles describes how the Vietcong, his former enemies, were motivated by a cause.

For men who had mounted commando raids on big American airfields, who had crawled through the barbed wire at American combat bases, who had been surrounded and escaped, war was the transcendent challenge . . . They believed they were fighting for a great goal, one worth dying for. Instead of working in the [rice] paddy, they were riding on the wind of history.

When people follow because of their dream, the psychology is called internalization. You follow because your individual goals are the same as the organization's or leader's goal. In other words, you and they believe in and want to make the same things happen. The staffer at the diabetes center and the follower of Fred Rogers had internalized shared goals and values. These followers control their ego drives and accept another's authority in their overriding desire to accomplish the goal. However, when the bond created by the dream withers, these people cease to play the follower role and the leader has no power over them.

When I was at Drake University, our basketball coach, Maury John, looked for dreamers. When recruiting players, he seldom discussed the scholarships or the other perks of college basketball. He never promised a player that he would start or be a star, though both were possibilities. Instead he focused on the dream—a chance to play on a team that went to the NCAA playoffs. If the recruit did not light up at this prospect, Maury John passed him over. He only wanted people who shared the dream—who were willing to follow to make it happen. For several years, Maury John produced highly cohesive teams that won championships, not individual stars.

For organizations to fully utilize these followers, they must be clear about their goals, the followers' goals, and how these two sets mesh. When giving out an assignment, leaders must show how it is tied to the goal. Likewise, when conflicts arise between the leader's view and the follower's view, use the overarching goal as the arbiter—that is, determine which view better serves achievement of the goal. Appeals to friendship, loyalty, or personal growth will generally fall on deaf ears.

These models represent some of the deliberate career choices those drawn to followership make. One other form of followership involves not only a career choice but also a way of life.

4. Enoughness

There is one other path of followership. It is taken by people who follow out of the conviction that no other lifeway is as rewarding. These people follow out of personal preference. For them, following is compatible with their personality. For example, they may be inherently altruistic, or naturally skilled at following, or the follower role may be most consistent with their outlook on life.

For some, following is a way of serving. This reason reaches back to the Old High German roots of the word "follower" that we traced earlier, that is, someone who helps, ministers to, or wants to be of service to another. Robert Greenleaf captures the spirit of this followership path in his remarkable book *Servant Leadership.*

> It begins with the natural feeling . . . deep down inside . . . that one wants to serve, to *serve first.* [That person is sharply different from one who is *leader first.*]
>
> The difference manifests itself in the care taken by the servant first to make sure that other people's highest priority needs are being served. The best test and most difficult to administer is: Do those served grow as persons? Do they, *while being served,* become healthier, wiser, freer, more autonomous, more likely themselves to become servants. [And what is the effect on the least privileged in society; will they benefit, or, at least, not be further deprived?]

Unlike followers who apprentice to get ahead, the primary interest of these followers is in helping others. I think of Mother Teresa and her sisters working in the slums of Calcutta or today's Peace Corps volunteers. Unlike their predecessors who were following the dream articulated by John F. Kennedy, many are trying to be of service to their Third World neighbors.

Greenleaf does not imply that servant-first people will never lead. In fact, some will be raised to leadership positions because others recognize and value this natural desire to serve others' interests. In the Catholic Church, priests are given the title Servant of God. Likewise, the Pope's actual title means the Servant of the Servants of God.

Rachel Carson, the author of *Silent Spring* and the founder of the modern-day environmental movement, never saw herself as a leader. Instead, she saw herself as a scientist and writer devoted to protecting our ecology. Yet her meticulous research, her ability to refute the propaganda of the chemical industry, and her dedication to our planet captured the imagination of young and old people alike. Because of her service, she was elevated to leadership and attracted many reformers who would defend everyone's right to a healthy world.

The Jewel Tea Company, one of America's largest grocery chains, adopted the following credo in their "first assistant philosophy" for their grocery store managers:

> Being a good first assistant means that each management person think of him- or herself not as the order-giving, domineering boss but as the first assistant to those who "report" to him or her in a more typical organizational sense. Thus we mentally turn our organizational charts upside down and challenge ourselves to seek ways in which we can . . . manage in the true democratic sense . . . that is, with the consent of the managed. Thus, the satisfactions . . . come from helping others to get things done and changed—and not from getting credit for doing and changing things ourselves.

Others consciously decide they are better suited to play the follower role all or part of the time. Dave Edmunds, an executive at a Fortune 100 pharmaceutical firm, decided this,

> After I finished college, this company put me, along with twenty-nine other graduates, in its two-year management training program. During those two years, I learned a lot about the company and my peers. This is a very competitive company. Everybody is always scrambling to get ahead. At the end of the two years, the twenty-five of us who were still left were set off in a horse race against each other.
>
> I realized that I did not want to spend my life competing against these folks for the next twenty-five to thirty years. Maybe I'm just not *that* competitive, but it did not seem like fun to me. Plus, I genuinely liked many of them and respected their skills. I thought about leaving the company, but then another thought struck me.
>
> My twenty-four peers who were setting out to be leaders would need good followers if they were to succeed. Rather than fighting with them, why didn't I offer to help them get what they wanted? After all, I had talents which could help them succeed. Wouldn't I be in a better position if these twenty-four were fighting over which one I would help? Effective followers who can operate independently and who can step in for the leader if need be are always in short supply. Rather than be a competitive, albeit friendly, threat, why not be a prized asset?

Shortly after that I realized that, in reality, we're all followers anyway. As a first-level supervisor, I'd be a follower to my manager, who is a follower to his department head. This continues all the way to the division president and beyond, with the CEO following the board of directors. If each of us is a follower at some level, why not put my efforts into being the best follower rather than focusing on leadership? It is all a matter of perspective, isn't it?

I've done very well for myself here, being promoted through the ranks to vice president. To the people under me, I'm a leader. But I have never coveted a leadership role. My career goals were to contribute to, rather than compete with, my colleagues—to earn their respect and trust. My promotions have resulted from good followership. More importantly, of the nine people left from training class, I'm the only one who is still friendly with all of them. Some are higher than me, some are lower. There are even people younger than me who passed me up. And I try to help them when I can. My strategy paid off for me. I avoided the struggle for leadership, kept my friends, and did a good job without constantly guarding against power and politics.

Jack Sumner, the executive vice president of a nonprofit hospital organization, also made such a choice.

To be perfectly honest, I'm uncomfortable being the leader. I don't mind having responsibility for representing this organization to its various publics. It's just that I don't like being the one that everybody looks to for a vision, or for inspiration, or for the final judgment. The pressure and visibility of the top spot are just a bit too much. I'm much better at giving input to the leader and helping the leader carry out objectives. Being the number two person suits me much better than being number one. It is the doing, not the directing, that turns me on.

Followers like Dave Edmunds and Jack Sumner exhibit a vital characteristic called "enoughness." This term comes from the Samoans. Although they were the first group to inhabit Hawaii, they were looked down upon by the settlers who came from America. The Samoans' view of life clashed with the Puritan work ethic. Since Samoans value the enjoyment of life more than they value working, they labor only as much as they must to let them live fully. If that requires only an hour each day, then so be it. This value, however, led to them being labeled lazy and undependable by others.

The Samoans hold another view. In their culture, the pervasive concept of enoughness guides their daily life. Once you have enough, you need no more, especially when it comes to work and material things. Anything, no matter how good or virtuous, when carried to an extreme will become a vice.

A good friend grew up in central India without the benefit of modern conveniences like refrigerators, stoves, or air conditioning. He had only one meal a day. If a protein-rich food, such as an egg, was available at the meal, most of the food went to whoever needed it. For instance, if a brother had a test that day in school, then he would get the protein to help him do better.

My friend once told me that coming to the United States as an adult was a mixed blessing. He enjoys the material comforts of the United States, but he misses the spirtual qualities of India. He believes we make too big a deal about the United States being a "developed" country, whereas India is supposedly "underdeveloped." We are an overdeveloped nation materially and an underdeveloped nation emotionally and spiritually, he contends. With the exception of promoting democracy, the United States has no higher purpose permeating its culture than making a buck. We spend an inordinate amount of time grasping for the outward signs of success and devote little to the meaning of life or caring for each other. As evidence, he cites the declining membership in religions and the fact that Americans send their elderly to nursing homes, children to day care, and spouses to therapists—all so we have time to pursue something "more important."

Many Americans cannot identify with the concept of enoughness or appreciate the importance of the spiritual side of life. We believe that more is better. How many of us have closets full of clothes we no longer wear, kitchen gadgets we seldom use, and furniture that we don't sit on. Acquisition of material things is a national pastime and a palliative for our anxieties. Somehow, they make us feel more secure. Before we even appreciate what we have, we're off acquiring more.

Perhaps the most intriguing followers who follow as a lifeway are those who have the instincts and habits of leaders but choose the follower role. These are people who may not have the time or emotional energy to take on another leadership role but still want to contribute. Some are leaders who know how important good followers are to them, and so they return the favor when they follow. Or perhaps their leadership talents are simply not suited to a particular situation, as when a leader in a private-sector firm feels like a fish out of water as a government leader, or a manufacturing leader may realize personal limitations in marketing.

Joann Black, the president of a midwestern bank, described her switch-hitting between both roles:

> There are more than enough opportunities in this world for followership and leadership. I try to find a balance between them because I find they complement each other well. Sometimes I like being out front. Other times I prefer letting someone else take the heat while I do my best to support her or him. Sometimes I like being the visionary. Other times I like toiling in the fields. When I lead, I try not to let my followers down. When I follow, I try not to let the leaders down.

Therefore, these individuals are followers because they have rationally decided that *following* is what they want to do. They realize that they will be happier and more synergy will occur if they complement rather than compete with the leader.

Organizations and leaders should respect and value individuals with these personal preferences. They should have jobs and assignments that build upon their altruism, their natural followership abilities, and their desired lifestyles. Even though talented, they should not be pushed into positions that are in conflict with who they are.

To some degree, every follower embodies some sense of enoughness—a valuable characteristic in these days of redefining work and life on a human scale more than on an organizational scale.

5. Identifying

Your Followership

Style

When I began giving seminars on followership, I was repeatedly asked about styles of followership, much as people are curious about the styles of leadership. For people to think of themselves as followers, they needed models that were dramatically different from the stereotypical passive sheep and yes-people. They needed models with whom to identify, in the same way students of leadership pore over models of Theory X, Y, and Z leaders.

Most people know their leadership style inside and out. If they care about succeeding in the role, they could ill afford to overlook it. The best leaders are attuned to themselves and their relationships with others —they understand who they are as leaders, what their strengths and weaknesses are in the role, and how they affect followers.

Yet these same people are woefully ignorant of their followership style. It is like people who have well-developed cognitive skills but no insight into their emotions. The imbalance can be catastrophic. Can you imagine a basketball player who shines on offense but has no defensive ability? What would an arm be if only the flexor muscles were fully developed while the extensor muscles were flaccid?

Since most of us spend the majority of our time in the followership role, it stands to reason that how we perform as followers determines, for the most part, how satisfied we are with our day-to-day work existence. Research has shown that people who do a great job at work generally feel better about their lives than people who are not happy with their work performance. Also, if our leaders and peers value us as great followers, we will get more positive feedback, opportunities for more challenging work, and concrete rewards.

Yet how can you do a great job following if you have little insight into how you carry out the role? This was the problem facing the participants in my workshops.

To address that problem, I developed a questionnaire. It has two specific purposes. First, it is meant to help people determine the kind of follower they are. Second, it will pinpoint one's strengths as a follower as well as identify those followership skills that need improving. It provides a road map for becoming a better apprentice, disciple, mentee, colleague, team member.

I present the questionnaire here for readers. In answering the questions, please be as accurate and frank as possible. Try not to deceive yourself by answering the way you think the best followers answer, or the way that you would like others to view you. This is a self-diagnostic instrument that no one but you will see. Think of it as video footage of your tennis swing. By documenting and analyzing the way you really follow, you can then begin improving your skills.

On the average, this test takes ten minutes to complete. Please take it before you read the rest of the chapter, so that you do not bias your answers.

X Followership Questionnaire

For each statement, please use the scale below to indicate the extent to which the statement describes you. Think of a specific but typical followership situation and how you acted.

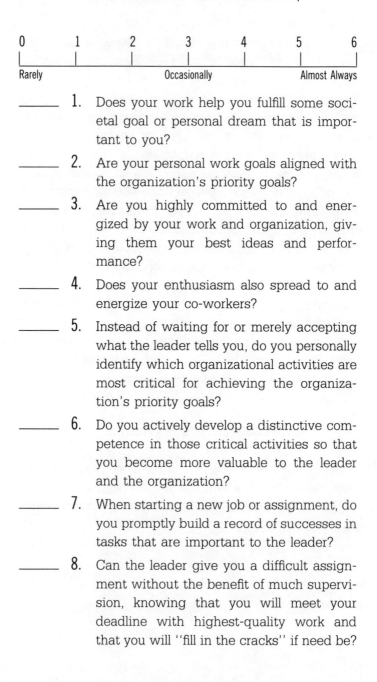

```
0       1       2       3       4       5       6
|_____|_____|_____|_____|_____|_____|
Rarely                Occasionally          Almost Always
```

_____ 1. Does your work help you fulfill some societal goal or personal dream that is important to you?

_____ 2. Are your personal work goals aligned with the organization's priority goals?

_____ 3. Are you highly committed to and energized by your work and organization, giving them your best ideas and performance?

_____ 4. Does your enthusiasm also spread to and energize your co-workers?

_____ 5. Instead of waiting for or merely accepting what the leader tells you, do you personally identify which organizational activities are most critical for achieving the organization's priority goals?

_____ 6. Do you actively develop a distinctive competence in those critical activities so that you become more valuable to the leader and the organization?

_____ 7. When starting a new job or assignment, do you promptly build a record of successes in tasks that are important to the leader?

_____ 8. Can the leader give you a difficult assignment without the benefit of much supervision, knowing that you will meet your deadline with highest-quality work and that you will "fill in the cracks" if need be?

90

_____ 9.   Do you take the initiative to seek out and successfully complete assignments that go above and beyond your job?

_____ 10. When you are not the leader of a group project, do you still contribute at a high level, often doing more than your share?

_____ 11. Do you independently think up and champion new ideas that will contribute significantly to the leader's or the organization's goals?

_____ 12. Do you try to solve the tough problems (technical or organizational), rather than look to the leader to do it for you?

_____ 13. Do you help out other co-workers, making them look good, even when you don't get any credit?

_____ 14. Do you help the leader or group see both the upside potential and downside risks of ideas or plans, playing the devil's advocate if need be?

_____ 15. Do you understand the leader's needs, goals, and constraints, and work hard to help meet them?

_____ 16. Do you actively and honestly own up to your strengths and weaknesses rather than put off evaluation?

_____ 17. Do you make a habit of internally questioning the wisdom of the leader's decision rather than just doing what you are told?

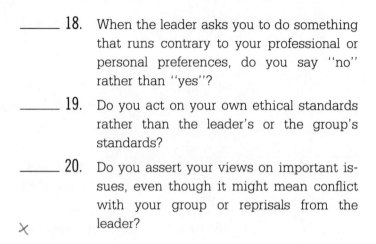

_____ 18. When the leader asks you to do something that runs contrary to your professional or personal preferences, do you say "no" rather than "yes"?

_____ 19. Do you act on your own ethical standards rather than the leader's or the group's standards?

_____ 20. Do you assert your views on important issues, even though it might mean conflict with your group or reprisals from the leader?

Developing a Key to Understanding Followers' Styles

Before you score the questionnaire to discover your followership style, let me briefly explain how the questionnaire was developed. In this way, you can understand what the questions above aim to discover about you.

Although numerous leadership-style questionnaires are available to the public, none had been developed for followership. I was starting from scratch. I could sit in my office, trying to pull items from academic sources, or I could get the needed information directly from followers and leaders. I chose the latter course.

When I asked people about followership styles, however, they gave me the expected stereotypical responses. Followers came in two styles: yes-people and sheep. To overcome these preconceived ideas, I took a different approach. I asked them to identify specific people in their organizations who represented the best followers in a positive sense, the worst ones, and the typical ones. I asked for in-depth descriptions of these individuals. What were they like as people? What did they do on the job that made them best, worst, or typical? What were the significant distinctions between each group? Why would they want to work with one follower and not another?

I asked the questions of individuals and focus groups. The similarity of results from group to group and person to person amazed me and the participants in my study. After culling out redundancies and rechecking, patterns began to emerge.

Two dimensions seemed to underlie the concept of followership. The first dimension is independent, critical thinking. The best followers are described as individuals who "think for themselves," "give constructive criticism," "are their own person," and "are innovative and creative." At the other end of the spectrum, the worst followers "must be told what to do," "can't make it to bathroom on their own," and "don't think." In between are the typical followers, who "take direction" and "don't challenge leader or group."

Alfred Adler demonstrated the independent thinking of the best followers in his relationship with Sigmund Freud. Adler was one of the first four people invited to form the Psychological Wednesday Society, the foundation from which psychoanalysis developed and spread. He cared deeply about the subject and about helping those with mental problems. Yet, unlike some of Freud's disciples, Adler had an "anti-doctrinaire nature [which] precluded him from swallowing systems whole . . . Though he acknowledged that

93

Sigmund's findings had opened new vistas, he had at the same time strained psychoanalysis and the realm of the unconscious through his own mind and declined to accept the entire credo." He made it clear that, although Freud was the pioneer, he was not giving up his own views or judgment. This trait made him a most valuable follower of Freud in the early years. It also allowed Adler to make his own major contributions to psychoanalysis, including the inferiority complex.

Compare Adler with leadership enthusiasts who believe that good followership means agreeing with the leader. A recent article in *Government Executive,* a management magazine for government workers, counsels would-be followers to "accept your boss's goals and objectives as your own." The message: Let the leader do the thinking and follow blindly, reinforcing the negative stereotype.

Yet independent thinking is only half of the followership equation. A review of best, worst, and typical followership characteristics reveals a second dimension: active engagement as a follower. The best followers "take initiative," "assume ownership," "participate actively," "are self-starters," and "go above and beyond the job." The worst ones are "passive," "lazy," "need prodding," "require constant supervision," and "dodge responsibility." The typical followers "get job done without supervision after told what to do," "CYA," and "shift with the wind."

Unlike leadership, followership appears to have a built-in paradox. Can people both think for themselves *and* actively accept the follower role? After all, doesn't accepting the role imply a willingness to follow orders— in other words, to let someone else do the thinking? As the next two chapters explain, exemplary followers have to balance these two requirements.

How do you rate on these two dimensions of followership—independent thinking and actively carrying out the role? That's what the test measures. What level of satisfaction do you find in each; how flexible are you in shifting from one extreme to the other?

X   Finding Your Followership Style

Let's return to the questionnaire. Use the scoring key below to score your answers to the questions.

Independent Thinking Items	SCORING	Active Engagement Items	SCORING
Question 1.	_____	Question 2.	_____
5.	_____	3.	_____
11.	_____	4.	_____
12.	_____	6.	_____
14.	_____	7.	_____
16.	_____	8.	_____
17.	_____	9.	_____
18.	_____	10.	_____
19.	_____	13.	_____
20.	_____	15.	_____
TOTAL SCORE	_____	TOTAL SCORE	_____

X

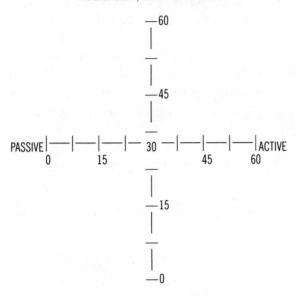

Add up your self-ratings on the Independent Thinking items. Mark the total on the vertical axis of the graph above. Repeat the procedure for the Active Engagement items and mark the total on the horizontal axis. Now plot your scores on the graph by drawing perpendicular lines connecting your two scores.

The juxtaposition of these two dimensions forms the basis upon which people classify followership styles. Five styles of followership emerge.

FIGURE 2.

Followership Styles

INDEPENDENT, CRITICAL THINKING

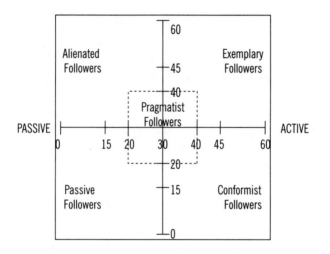

DEPENDENT, UNCRITICAL THINKING

Followership Style	Independent Thinking Score	Active Engagement Score
EXEMPLARY	High	High
ALIENATED	High	Low
CONFORMIST	Low	High
PRAGMATIST	Middling	Middling
PASSIVE	Low	Low

Now look at yourself via the mirror of the questionnaire. In which quadrant of Figure 2 do you fall? Locating your position on Figure 2 yields two benefits. First, you can identify your current followership style. You can now turn to the description of each style in the next section of this chapter to learn about your style in more detail. Second, you have a road map indicating what you can personally do to improve your followership skills. Thus the results of the questionnaire are both descriptive and prescriptive.

Please keep in mind that these labels categorize how you carry out the followership role, not who you are as a person. At any point in time, or under different circumstances, you may use one followership pattern rather than another. For example, inexperienced followers may change their styles over their careers as they gain more experience and confidence. Or if you have a mean-spirited, authoritarian boss, you may choose to alter your followership style to protect yourself. Likewise, followership in crises or stressful times, like the Bhopal disaster, might require a shift in style. But these tend to be exceptions. The point is to understand what pattern you typically use and why you use it.

Let's turn now to the descriptions of each followership style. As you read them, think of your own experiences as a follower. Determine the extent to which your style captures your feelings, attitudes, and behaviors while in the role. The following section describes all the followership styles except the exemplary followership style, which is fleshed out in later chapters.

The Alienated Follower

Are you someone whose positive self-image includes:

- Being a maverick who thinks for yourself?
- Having a healthy skepticism that sees things for what they really are?
- Playing the devil's advocate in the group?
- Being the organizational conscience?
- Sticking up for the little person?

Yet have you picked up from others that they don't always share your perception? In fact, do some people, especially leaders, view you as:

- Troublesome, cynical, or negative?
- Having a chip on your shoulder—a rebel without a cause?
- Headstrong and lacking judgment?
- Not a team player?
- Adversarial to the point of being hostile?

Are you disgruntled with your situation because you feel the leader or the organization:

- Does not fully recognize or utilize your talents and ideas?
- Exploited you for their gain but not yours?
- Has let you down by not holding up their end of the bargain?
- Is not aboveboard in their dealings with you or others?

- Refuses to acknowledge their shortcomings and inconsistencies?

If these descriptions fit you, you are an alienated follower. You continue to think independently and critically, but you are not very active in carrying out the role. In fact, you might find yourself disengaging at times.

Hawkeye Pierce, in the TV series M*A*S*H, personified the 15 to 25 percent of followers who are alienated. Capable but cynical, alienated followers sarcastically criticize the leader's efforts, frequently hold back their own effort, or sink gradually into disgruntled acquiescence.

Most alienated followers began as exemplary ones. Somehow, sometime, something turned them off, resulting in withdrawal. They see themselves as victims who unfairly got the short end of the stick.

They are hurt or angry, wanting to punish someone for it. Any emotional energy is channeled into fighting *against* those parts of the present organization that they dislike rather than *toward* their work or a desired future. In fact, punishment is often an emotional precondition to focusing on solutions or positively pursuing a dream of what might be.

In reality, though, this punishment may never set things right. By badgering the leader or organization, they create conditions for retaliation. Reassignments and forced firings are not uncommon fates for alienated followers.

Barry Paris, the biographer of Greta Garbo and silent film star Louise Brooks, is an interesting case study in alienation. For over ten years, he wrote for Pittsburgh's morning newspaper, the *Post-Gazette,* and was hired, fired, and rehired more times than he cares to remember. According to former colleagues, much of Paris' problem was his attitude.

"Everybody on a newspaper staff has to do some things that he or she doesn't particularly want to do, because they're part of what we sell," said George Anderson, former *Post-Gazette* magazine editor.

"Barry only wanted to do the things that interested him. He never refused an assignment, but he was clearly less enthusiastic about doing things that didn't particularly appeal to him. He had a hard time working as part of the team or under any supervision."

According to *Post-Gazette* editor John G. Craig, Jr., "[Barry's] very self-centered. Maybe that's a characteristic of people who are talented in the way that he's talented. I do think his talent is sometimes greater than his judgment, however."

Let's now hear Barry Paris' side of the story.

"I finally realized that the newspaper business is full of the same hypocrisies that characterize business and politics," Paris says. "The major hypocrisy is the phony concept of objectivity. It's a fine ideal, a standard to which people maybe should aspire, but it's one that's virtually never realized.

"People who are better adjusted than I learn how to deal with such things in a comfortable and successful way," Paris adds. "I could never resign myself to it. I'd brood and fume. Looking back, what a waste of time it all was. I took all of it much too seriously."

Alienated followers like Barry Paris are deeply unhappy about their work situation. They direct their resulting hostility toward the boss or the "system," lashing out whenever they get a chance, regardless of how appropriate or effective it might be. Seldom do they succeed at changing anything, which simply adds more fuel to their burning unhappiness. Life seems unfair, and the only way to maintain their self-esteem is to confront the cause or withdraw emotionally. In either case, as Paris concluded, such brooding is a waste of time, making for a life that is not richly lived.

Eventually, alienated followers cause resentment in the leader and other followers who can make life increasingly difficult for them. Either they resign themselves to going through the steps halfheartedly or they quit to go off on their own or find an organization that will value them.

The Causes of Alienation

What gives rise to alienated followers? The answer often depends on whom you ask. Traditionally, only the leader was consulted and his or her word was accepted as truth. For example, an executive at Intel described an alienated subordinate: "Jones is a talented guy and his skills are critical to our project. But ever since he came into the department, he's had a chip on his shoulder. He thinks he's right and has an opinion on everything. If I criticize his work, he bristles. At meetings, he's sarcastic as hell in front of my group, always picking apart everything I say. It's like he's got this thing against authority figures. Maybe he's had bad supervisors in the past. I've tolerated him up to now because I need his output. Once this project's over, I'm putting him on notice: walk the straight and narrow or pack up your desk."

Granted, we all know a few people whose personalities ooze cynicism and dissatisfaction. But they do not constitute most of the 15 to 25 percent of the population that are alienated followers. When I queried followers, I found that their alienation frequently resulted from unmet expectations and broken trust. One follower at Data General in Boston explained: "Last year I was assigned to this high-priority project. My supervisor told me it was a 'showstopper' project for our division. The people who dedicated themselves to it would go places in the company and get extra bonuses. The pressure was intense from the start. For months, I worked sixty- to seventy-hour weeks, often coming in both Saturday and Sunday. I traveled weekly to meet with the customer. Needless to say, my family life paid the price.

"After nine months, the division pulled the plug on the project with no warning to those of us who gave it our all. The product we were making was one of the best I've seen in this company. But they cut it off before it had a chance. Now I feel that those of us connected to the project are seen as losers. I asked my boss about the extra bonuses. She said to forget it. They were history.

"I've since been assigned to another project. They're looking for new ideas and I've got some, especially from what we learned. But it's hard for me to gear up for it. I'll admit it. I'm dragging my feet because I feel so let down."

The lack of trust is a major issue for followers. In one survey, I found that followers could identify only two out of five of the managers in their work experience as being able to instill trust or confidence. Followers trust their direct managers about two-thirds of the time and top management only about half the time.

Leaders who exploit followers for their own personal gain can expect hostility directed back at them. Or a leader may simply mismanage a worker so badly that alienation results. Alienation also occurs when leaders or organizations switch goals on their followers, replacing mutually shared ones with goals that followers don't believe in.

Alienation also stems from unmet expectations. My survey revealed that despite high performance, groups and individuals failed to be recognized for their contributions about two-thirds of the time. Likewise, the company failed to capitalize on their ideas at least one-third of the time. As one alienated follower told me, "If my boss isn't going to use my ideas, why bother?" In this age of downsizing and restructuring, respondents believe their companies are loyal to them only 66 percent of the time.

Since most alienated followers began as exemplary ones, returning to that style requires confronting the perceived inequity. If trust was broken, it must be reestablished. If expectations are unmet, they must be addressed. If goals diverged, they need to be realigned, perhaps by finding an overarching goal that both parties can accept. Without these actions, the alienation will undoubtedly persist.

From a personal viewpoint, continuing to vent your hostility over the broken trust and unmet expectations generally leads nowhere. Although you may feel moments of satisfaction from getting a jab in here or there, it is ultimately a losing proposition. You are unhappy and you are making others unhappy both at work and at home.

Think of what it is like to live with alienated follow-

ers. They come home from work griping and sniping.
Chances are this dominates their mood at home, thus
depriving them of relief and the positive affection they
so desperately want. They probably have little patience
and explode over small things, which further distances
them from their loved ones.

Even if they can leave their hostility at work, they
are developing a Jekyll and Hyde personality. This puts
them at a health risk. As Daniel Goleman reported in   EI
The New York Times Magazine, psychologists have
found that "people who are chronically hostile, who see
the world through a lens of suspicion and cynicism, are
particularly vulnerable to heart disease." Goleman isn't
just talking about people who bang the table or start
fights. "More subtle types of hostility—skepticism, mistrust, a propensity to make snide comments—are just
as damaging."

Your choices are to remain unhappy, leave before
getting fired, or move to another style. From the perspective of my research, the viable choice is exemplary
followership. Sinking into disgruntled acquiescence will
not relieve your anger. Becoming a conformist would
cost you your independent, critical thinking—a steep
price which is unproductive for you and the organization. Only exemplary followership gives a constructive
outlet that can transform the energy of your anger into a
positive force.

Moving from Alienated to Exemplary Followership   Greg

To become exemplary, you already possess one of the
two important dimensions: independent, critical thinking. Your problem is overcoming your negativity and
becoming actively engaged once again.

Think back on what it was like as an exemplary follower before you become alienated. How did you carry out the role? If you are like other exemplary followers, then you were very focused on the dream. What was it that you wanted to make happen as a follower? If you still believe in it, then perhaps you can accept that setbacks are part of reaching any goal.

Everyone gets battered about occasionally in organizations. But letting it keep you from both goal achievement and day-to-day work satisfaction is to get robbed twice. Broken trust and unmet expectations, although painful, should not also deprive you of the energy or the satisfaction of achieving your goal.

It is not just a matter of your "rights" being violated. If you belong to a community or organization, you have certain responsibilities. One is to contribute to making it better for everyone, not just yourself. To the extent that you stay physically but withdraw emotionally, you are taking up resources that someone else might better use.

The best way to overcome your hostility toward the leader is to confront it and then replace it with something more positive. If you trust your boss, sit down and lay your cards out on the table. Let your boss know how you feel, and what you would like to happen to remedy the situation. Listen to your boss's perspective, especially what parts of you are problematic. Own up to your contribution to the problem. Then try to reach a mutually satisfactory resolution of past grievances.

If you can't trust your boss, then transfer to a new organizational unit or find a job with a new company. Get a fresh start by leaving behind the old emotional baggage. At the onset, negotiate reasonable expectations for both sides.

Whether you work things out with your old boss or a new one, you must find something positive that engages you, something that pulls your energy back into the followership role. In most cases, this is a mutually shared dream or goal. To the extent that you harness your talents toward a future that you and the leader want to make happen, rather than focusing your energy against the leader, you are on the road to exemplary followership again.

The Conformist

Do you and leaders view your positive attributes as:

- Accepting assignments easily and gladly doing the work?
- Team playing?
- Trusting and committing yourself to the leader or the organization?
- Minimizing conflict?
- Being nonthreatening to the leader?

But have you also gotten feedback from co-workers, your spouse, or even the leader that you are also seen as:

- Lacking your own ideas?
- Obsequious and self-deprecating?
- Unwilling to take an unpopular position and stick to it?
- Averse to conflict, even at the risk of going over the cliff with the group?
- Compromising your or your family's needs and ideas to please the organization?

People with the above characteristics often find themselves working in environments where:

- Following the established order is more important than outcomes.
- A domineering leader or culture presides.
- Disagreeing with the supervisor or making waves is punished.
- Uniformity of dress, behavior, and attitudes is encouraged.

If the above describes your situation, you are probably a conformist follower. For example, do you find yourself often saying "yes" when you really want to say "no"? Or, like Oliver North, who testified during the Iran-Contra hearings, are you "not in the habit of questioning your superiors"? You may think this is what is expected of followers. But it is not. As shall become clear, it doesn't serve you and it also doesn't serve the organization.

The opposite of alienated followers, conformists score high on the active engagement scale but low on independent thinking. This suggests that this 20 to 30 percent of the population feels comfortable in the follower role. That's good, but the problem is that these followers turn over too much of the thinking to the leader.

Conformists are all too eager to take orders, to defer to the leader's authority, and to yield to the leader's views or judgments. They assume that the leader's position of power entitles him or her to obedience and accommodation from the subordinate. Conformists know their place and do not question the social order. They find comfort in structure and in having someone above them. They are the consummate "good child," all too eager to please the boss/parent.

The Causes of Conformism

Erich Fromm, the renowned psychoanalyst, explored conformism in *Escape from Freedom*. He wondered why both Germany's and Italy's citizens surrendered their hard-won but young democracies to embrace fascism during the 1930s.

Fromm discovered that some people find freedom terrifying. Freedom poses too many choices and too much uncertainty. They find difficult the responsibility to make and live with a choice. They desire structure, order, and predictability, but the task of creating their own in the face of freedom is overwhelming. Being overwhelmed makes them feel powerless and afraid. To counteract these feelings, they seek escape. They turn to anyone who offers to remove the burden of freedom. This is especially true if the whole societal fabric starts to unravel, as it did in Germany and Italy during the 1920s and 1930s, and as seems to be happening in corporate America in the 1990s.

But a dependent personality is not the whole story. Most societies encourage conformity. Submission to authority is reinforced at home, in schools, at church, on sports teams, in the military, and at work. The rationale is that the price of victory—whether in life, war, or merely a basketball game—is deference to authority. To win requires speed and decisiveness with no room for debate or democracy. To succeed, followers must just do what they are told.

Red Auerbach, formerly coach and now president

of the Boston Celtics basketball team, espoused this view. When he read my article "In Praise of Followers" in the *Harvard Business Review,* he responded, "Can you imagine a team in which players picked other players and decided on the substitutions? It is absolutely ludicrous. Or can you imagine a business run by people without authority or by people who are not in a position to assume the responsibility of failure? Can a ship be run without a captain? It would undoubtedly flounder."

I was actually surprised by Auerbach's ungenerous reaction to the concept of followership. His team's creativity and spontaneity on the court seem to belie his words. Perhaps he issues the overall commands, but they definitely carry them out with great individuality and independence. When they lose, they seem as downcast and responsible as Auerbach. An objective observer, I think, would notice a sizeable discrepancy between Auerbach's words and reality.

Now, I'm not suggesting that a democratic vote on each decision is appropriate when you are pinned down by enemy fire. In the heat of battle, we want people to carry out their orders swiftly and effectively. But, we don't need to breed conformists to achieve that goal. In fact, the most effective teams exercise participation up front by having members contribute to and critique the plans before the battle. Their resulting confidence in and commitment to the plan, then, enables them to carry it out with precision.

Domineering leaders who seek power over others encourage conformists. Whether their dominance is expressed through charisma or authoritarianism, they need yes-people to feel fulfilled. They are like magnets in search of iron filings. If the filing is not magnetized, they will set about doing it.

These leaders can exact a high price for noncon-formance. This further encourages conformist behavior. Quick punishment and reprisals occur when you fail to be magnetized. People learn to distort the truth to keep the peace.

Likewise, the rules and rigid procedures of some bureaucracies, whether government, philanthropic, reli-gious, or business, attract and spawn conformists. Even office environments reinforce conformism. The offices of a major oil company I visited illustrates this. In every office, the desk faces the same way, a piece of modern art hangs on the wall behind the desk, and a small white plastic pot on a corner of the desk holds an indoor plant.

Why, I asked my host, were all the offices so much alike?

She said that the company had an office standards policy. Employees are unable to rearrange their furni-ture because desks and cabinets are built into the walls. If they are interested in greenery, they are generously permitted to supply their own—if, that is, the plants are placed in the white pots that management approves. If they are interested in art, they have no recourse what-ever. They may neither decorate their own spaces nor remove the modern paintings that adorn all offices and halls. They are allowed a photo, but only of family and no larger than five by seven.

The company's office standards committee moni-tors periodically and places notes in the personnel files of those who do not comply. This company, like so many similarly misguided organizations, has mandated a sterilized, standardized environment in which any in-dividual impulses or influences are speedily sup-pressed.

The irony is that the purpose of my visit was to help them improve creativity and innovation in the work force.

The paradox facing this oil company is at the nub of the problem with conformist followership. The world is too complex for leaders to maneuver single-handedly. For your organization to thrive in the face of global competition requires followers to be more than enthusiastic carbon copies of the leader. You must contribute all your talents, especially your brainpower, to the enterprise.

After all, which company would you expect to spot new market trends, seek and utilize customer input, innovate new products, come up with new ways to manufacture, have a highly actualized work force, and fight off competitors from all continents? A company with one leader who does all the thinking and whose five hundred active followers simply echo him or her? Or a company with a thinking leader and five hundred thinking and actively engaged followers?

Conformism adds very little value in today's rapidly changing world. In more stable times, conformity has less downside. In fact, it helped grease the wheels of efficiency. Much research has demonstrated that homogeneous groups perform well on routine, highly structured problems. But given complex or turbulent problems, homogeneous groups fall flat on their face. Heterogeneous groups with conflicting views and diverse styles do much better. Out of the clash of differences comes the creative solution needed.

Conformists lack what St. Theresa of Avila, the 16th century mystic, called the precondition for following: an informed intellect. She reminded would-be disciples that without an intellectual foundation and sound judgment, you have no basis for your leap of faith. To keep her mystical pursuits in check and on track, she reached this conclusion: "If I have to choose, let me have as a confessor a theologian rather than a saint." She understood the value of someone who would challenge her belief system rather than reinforce it.

Being a conformist follower affects you personally. You lose credibility when you don't think for yourself. Although some leaders may value your attributes, others do not see you as a full contributor. You will not be seen as someone who can operate independently or who could ever take over the leadership role.

Also, controlling your anxiety through conformism is an ultimately losing proposition. In a world turning upside down, conformism imposes a false sense of order. Like a talisman to ward off your uncomfortable feelings, conformity keeps you from confronting the reality of change. By trying to avoid conflict, you sow the seeds of your own unhappiness. Your lack of inner resolve creates a mixture of anxiety, guilt, and self-reproach. In the process, you make yourself vulnerable to unscrupulous leaders who prey on your anxiety.

You also need to consider the effect of your conformism on your family. While focusing on your responsibility to authority, you often neglect your responsibilities to your family and yourself. When you are unable to say "no" to your boss's request that you work late, then they will not see you. Plus, you will probably try to homogenize their life experience, as you try to conform to the "standards" of your community. In the process, your children will either model themselves after you or rebel and become alienated. In either case, you have not opened them up to a more viable alternative to conformism—that is, exemplary followership.

Moving from Conformist to Exemplary Followership

To shift from a conformist style to an exemplary style, you are well positioned. You are already seen as a committed contributor, someone who is actively engaged. To become a full contributor, you need to cultivate independent, critical thinking and develop the courage to exercise it. This involves gaining confidence in your own views and realizing that the organization needs your views.

The question facing you is how to accomplish this transformation. The first step is to begin evaluating others' ideas. Try to understand what they want to accomplish, then weigh the pros and cons of the idea vis-à-vis the goal. Learn to play the devil's advocate who asks the tough questions about the idea's feasibility. Spot the shortcomings so that they can be dealt with before implementing the idea, rather than after the fact.

Next, start generating your own ideas. What do you think will help achieve the organization's goal? How could you make the work more efficient? Are some implementation plans more effective than others? By what criteria?

Finally, confront your fear of conflict and need for structure. These emotional issues need resolving before you can become fully independent or disagree with the leader. This is easier said than done. Some people will not be able to achieve it without professional help.

A starting point is to simply watch what happens when other people disagree with each other or the leader. How do they go about it? Are they blunt or tactful? Are they tuned in to each other's feelings or self-centered? Are they flexible and willing to offer alternatives or do they rigidly stand behind only one solution?

Then notice what happens after the conflict. Is the outcome better as a result of the disagreement? Is there a mutually satisfactory resolution or winners and losers? Do the losers feel and act like losers or do they feel good that they expressed their views even if their views didn't win out? Do both sides retain respect for each other after the outcome? Is everyone committed to carrying out the outcome with enthusiasm?

What you will probably discover is that the world seldom falls apart due to conflict. In fact, conflict often clears the air so that real progress can be made. It brings smoldering problems to the surface so that they can be dealt with in an open and direct way.

Try to piece together what you learn into a style that works for you. Then experiment. Pick an area where you have expertise. Then, the next time you have an idea or you disagree with someone about that area, raise it. See what happens. Chances are you will not only survive but also get positive feedback about your contribution. Even if you get shot down, don't give up. Keep experimenting. Try another approach next time. After a few tries, you will find one that works. Then keep practicing.

The goal is twofold. On the one hand, you want to be valued as a full contributor. On the other hand, you want to free yourself from the constraints of your own insecurity. In today's world, being able to stand on your own two feet is a necessity, since you never know when events will cast you adrift in the seas of change.

The Pragmatist

Are you someone who sees the positive aspects of your followership style as:

- Being attuned to the shifting winds of organizational politics?
- Knowing how to work the system to get things done?
- Keeping things in perspective?
- Toeing the middle line so as to keep the organization from going overboard in either direction?
- Playing by the rules and regulations?

Yet do others sometimes interpret these in a negative light and see you as:

- Playing political games?
- Bargaining to maximize your own self-interest?
- Being averse to risk and prone to cover your tracks?
- Carrying out your assignments with middling enthusiasm and in a mediocre fashion?
- Being a bureaucrat who adheres to the letter of the rule rather than the spirit?

When you assess your work environment, do you find:

- High uncertainty and instability with everchanging orders and agendas?
- An impersonal climate between bosses and subordinates?

- An active, buzzing grapevine?
- A transactional atmosphere where people have to cut deals to get things done?
- An emphasis on staying within the rules and regulations?

If you see yourself in these descriptions, then you can count yourself among the 25 to 35 percent who use the pragmatist followership style. Pragmatists hug the middle of the road. They question their leader's decisions, but not too often or too critically. They perform their required tasks, but seldom venture beyond them.

The Cause of Pragmatism

Why do people adopt a pragmatist style? Some leaders suggest that pragmatists are sensitive to political shifts, that they are gamespeople who manipulate others and the organization to their benefit. They avoid taking a strong position that crosses powerful people. They keep conflict to a minimum and always have a ready excuse with a corresponding paper trail for any failure.

Other leaders explain that these followers have a low risk tolerance, living by the slogan "Better safe than sorry." They want to do a good job, but they are not willing to stick their necks out, or worse, to fail. They set their sights low and make sure others sign off before they do.

However, I have found that the pragmatist style is as much influenced by the leader and the organization as by personality. Often it is a coping response to an unstable situation, either organizationally or politically.

In the government, political appointees often come and go at a fast clip. These temporary leaders usually have their own political agendas and personal idiosyncrasies. They often try to bring about significant changes in a short time. Via cajoling or bullying, they enlist the permanent civil servants in the implementation of their goals. Yet government careerists who have been around a while understand that no sooner will they begin implementing the "agenda du jour" than a new person will move into the top spot. They respond to this revolving door much the same way sailors deal with tides. They anchor far enough away from shore so as not to get beached, yet close enough to harbor so as not to capsize in a storm.

Pragmatism also emerges when the organization itself becomes unstable. In 1989, when Kodak restructured for the fourth time in six years, many of its employees hunkered down into the survivor mode amid the confusion and dampening morale. With the announcement that 4,500 people were to be fired, many started covering their tracks to avoid the pink slip.

Finally, leaders themselves can encourage pragmatism in followers. Leaders who play games or politics with their subordinates can expect the same in return. Leaders who are impersonal, putting tremendous emotional distance between themselves and their followers, will find followers not committing themselves one way or the other. And leaders who have transactional relationships with people, where everything is tit for tat, elicit the same from followers. With all of these leadership styles, pragmatism becomes both a rational and a safe choice for followers.

The Downside of Pragmatism

Regardless of how you became a pragmatist, you need to understand its downside. The discrepancy between one's own and others' perceptions limits the pragmatist's effectiveness. Others won't trust her and will suspect her motives. She may be kept out of important decision loops and not get plum assignments.

Being in a pragmatist mode also takes its personal toll. If the dominant emotions of the alienated follower are hurt and anger, then pragmatists feel complacency mixed with anxiety. Complacency comes from being on automatic pilot and doing less than they are capable. Neither out front nor dragging up the rear, they are safe in the middle, increasing their sense of security by using office politics to protect themselves.

The anxiety results from not knowing whom to trust or feeling safe enough to let defenses down. Keeping up constantly with organizational politics drains much energy from the enjoyment of life. Monitoring the grapevine, building alliances, and protecting their flanks all consume time and effort. Since their work load will take up much of the workday, the extra time comes out of their personal life. Strategizing for self-defense becomes a constant necessity and a burden.

The major justification for retaining a pragmatist style is that, for the most part, it works. After all the worry, plotting, and game playing, pragmatists traditionally hold on to their jobs, even after others are let go. They might not get promoted, but they also are not the first to get fired.

Moving from Pragmatism to Exemplary Followership

The question facing these followers, though, is whether surviving is enough. Isn't life and time too valuable to be wasted away on mediocrity? Dante wrote in the *Inferno,* "The hottest places in hell are reserved for those who . . . maintain their neutrality." Neither God nor the devil wanted those who live life in the middle, refusing to commit themselves.

If you are a pragmatist, besides protecting yourself, isn't there something you want to accomplish in life? Is there a goal you can commit yourself to with enthusiasm?

Goals can transform people. As we shall see in the next chapters, they can turn mediocre followers into exemplary ones. This can happen at any stage in life.

Consider the story of Ray Kroc. Most people focus on his life after he became CEO of McDonald's, as if that is when he became noteworthy. Of equal fascination is what happened before he was CEO, when he was in the followership role.

Until he was fifty-two years old, Ray Kroc bounced from job to job, giving and getting little from each one. As a middling traveling salesperson hawking milkshake machines in 1955, he came across a new fast-food chain that captured his imagination. It was a turning point in his life. At the age of fifty-two and after years of surviving, Ray Kroc had found his purpose.

For six years he worked for the McDonald brothers as a franchising agent, expanding the chain from 30 to 200 stores. He was turned on, contributing all his tal-

ents to the enterprise—his ideas, his energy, his enthusiasm. According to Dick McDonald, "he was dynamic
. . . aggressive . . . He was more enthused about the
prospects than my brother and me."

Here was this man in his fifties, by all accounts a
classic pragmatist, who was probably thinking of retirement. Then he finds his purpose and it transforms him
from a pragmatist to an exemplary follower. For six
years, he gives his all, while the McDonald brothers are
getting rich and building an empire. Sure, he got the
opportunity to buy them out, but the story did not have
to end that way. If it hadn't, it would in no way diminish the power of finding a purpose that transforms you
or the value of his six years of exemplary followership.
Those six years probably meant more to Kroc than the
previous thirty years of work.

Once pragmatists find a purpose, they must also
build up the trust and credibility that overcome the
negative perceptions that people hold about them. One
approach is to help other people achieve their goals,
rather than always looking out for number one first. Try
to understand what your colleagues and your leader
want to accomplish. Then put your underutilized talents
—particularly your brainpower and enthusiasm—to
work for them. Do not forget that your considerable talent at working the system can be a real plus when used
for more than your individual self-interest.

The Passive Follower

When you are in the follower role, do you believe you
should:

- Rely on the leader's judgment and thinking?
- Take action only when the boss gives instructions?
- Let the people who get paid for it handle the headaches?

Have your co-workers or your boss grumbled about your work performance, indicating that you:

- Are only putting in your time but little else?
- Don't do your share?
- Require an inordinate amount of supervision relative to your contribution?
- Follow the crowd without considering why?

When you think about your work situation, do you believe:

- The organization doesn't want your ideas?
- The leader is going to do what she or he wants?
- Going along with the boss and the group is your only choice?
- Effort and contribution don't get you anywhere?

If these adjectives capture your views of followership, then you are a passive follower—a member of the smallest minority, about 5 to 10 percent of the population. Passive followers are the exact opposite of exemplary followers. At the extreme, they look to the leader to do their thinking, and they do not carry out their assignments with enthusiasm. Lacking in initiative and a sense of responsibility, they require constant direction when performing the tasks given them and never venture beyond their assignment.

Becoming a Passive Follower

Yet, for those who adopt a passive style of followership, how does it happen? Leaders like to attribute the cause to the personality of the follower. They describe passive followers as lazy, incompetent, unmotivated, or downright stupid. They can't tell the difference between the letter and the spirit of a command.

In the extreme, passive followers may have a herd instinct—like sheep. We generally think of these people as mindless and rudderless, followers who latch on to a leader.

A few people do fit these stereotypes. Yet my research and experience show that many passive followers are simply people who haven't developed their followership skills. So they basically do nothing. Other passive followers don't like being in the follower role. When they find themselves in it, they shut down, expending as little thought or effort as possible.

Passive following is often a response to leader expectations. When leaders treat followers like sheep, they will generally get what they expect. Red Auerbach of the Boston Celtics wrote, "In any team situation, followers will not create, they will not take the blame, and they will not experiment because of the possibility of making mistakes." When a leader sends this message, some followers will make sure the boss is right. They will gladly allow the boss to carry the full burdens of thinking and motivation. This is especially true if the boss has not recognized or rewarded the followers' own thinking or motivation in the past.

This often occurs when leaders feel a need to con-

123

trol every situation and use fear to keep the followers in line. Leaders who assign all goals, make every decision, watch over people's shoulders, or persistently prod will find some followers sliding into the passive role.

Moving from Passive to Exemplary Followership

This transformation requires learning the range of followership skills. It means understanding that following is neither a mindless, passive activity nor a spectator sport. To do it well means investing and involving yourself.

But rather than go into great detail here, let's turn to the next chapter, which describes exemplary followers and the specifics of what they do.

6. The Skills

of Exemplary

Followers

Exemplary followers are different from other followers in that they perform well on both underlying dimensions of followership. On the one hand, they exercise independent, critical thinking, separate from the leader or the group. Leaders and co-workers describe them as "thinking for themselves." They "are their own persons," they are "innovative and creative," "give constructive criticism," and "are willing to stand up to leaders."

On the other hand, exemplary followers are actively engaged, applying their talents for the benefit of the organization even when confronted with bureaucratic inanities or nonproducing co-workers. It is said that they "take initiative," "assume ownership," "participate actively," "are self-starters," "support team and leader" "are extremely competent," and "go above and beyond the job."

Exemplary followers balance these two seemingly mutually exclusive requirements. They have to. Independent thinking without active engagement can lead people with great ideas to fall short of implementing them or to become smart cynics who harass the leader. Active engagement without independent thinking can lead to yes-people who uncritically accept orders, whether good or bad. But exemplary followers who use both these skills become enormously valuable to leaders and their organizations. Many leaders will go to great lengths to attract and accommodate exemplary followers because their contribution is both different and better.

For example, King Henry VIII emphasizes these differences in Robert Bolt's play *A Man for All Seasons.* When Henry VIII decides to divorce his wife and marry his mistress, thus breaking with the Catholic Church, he seeks the approval of Sir Thomas More, Lord Chancellor of England. Although unquestionably loyal to the king, Thomas More finds he cannot support either the divorce or the schism. In a turning-point scene, Henry pleads with Thomas More to go along with him.

"Thomas, how is it that you cannot see? Everyone else does."

"Then why does Your Grace need my poor support?" More asks.

"Because you are honest. What's more to the purpose, you're known to be honest . . . There are those, like Norfolk, who follow me because I wear the crown, and there are those like Master Cromwell who follow me because they are jackals with sharp teeth and I am their lion, and there is a mass that follow me because it follows anything that moves—and there is you."

"I am sick to think how much I displease Your Grace."

"No, Thomas, I respect your sincerity. Respect? Oh, man, it's water in the desert . . ."

In this brief exchange, Henry VIII pinpoints what makes exemplary followership stand out from the other four styles—independent thinking while remaining actively engaged as a follower. Thomas More's judgment is valuable to Henry VIII precisely because Thomas thinks for himself rather than bends to pressure. He doesn't give in to curry favor with the king or to avoid his wrath.

At the same time, Henry knows that Thomas is devoted to him. Unlike Cromwell, he is not trying to assume the king's power. He gladly plays the follower role, using his talents to promote the country's best interests. Rather than withdraw or submit against his conscience, he actively engages the king in dialogue to help the king see the error of his ways.

Exemplary followers put their talents, including their brainpower, to work for the organization and its leaders—sometimes complementing the leader's efforts and other times relieving the leader of many tasks. Less effective followers fail in this dimension because they halfheartedly go through the motions.

Consider how Michael Eisner, the CEO of Walt Disney Co., views one of his best followers. Says Eisner, "[He] is a great devil's advocate. I mean, he will ask the questions nobody ever thought of, and he will take the opposite side of everything. But he is a deal maker, not a deal breaker and that's very unique." This follower's value to Eisner is that his thinking is directed at producing successful outcomes for the organization.

In some ways, the seeming paradox facing followers is the flip side of the one facing leaders. Today's leaders are expected to take charge and yet transfer authority and responsibility to subordinates. How can they be in charge if followers have the power? The answer is that exemplary followers give a leader their best thinking, thus complementing the leader's own strengths. By being actively engaged these followers can increase rather than sap a leader's power.

The Skills of Exemplary Followers

As I listened to people describe exemplary followers, I wanted more detail. What was meant by "think for themselves," "go above and beyond the job," or "support the team and the leader"? How do these qualities manifest themselves in the day-to-day activities of the best followers? Can the skills of exemplary followers be taught to others?

To answer these questions I probed exemplary followers, their leaders, and their co-workers. Through interviews, workshops, and questionnaires, they spelled out in detail what exemplary followers do that sets them apart from their colleagues. After several iterations of the process, common themes emerged.

Exemplary followers possess a repertoire of skills and values that are both learnable and doable. These can be divided into three broad categories:

- Job Skills—how exemplary followers add value with their:
    - Focus and commitment
    - Competence in critical path activities
    - Initiative in increasing their value to the organization
- Organizational Skills—how exemplary followers nurture and leverage a web of organizational relationships with:
    - Team members
    - Organizational networks
    - Leaders
- Values Component—how exemplary followers exercise a courageous conscience which guides their job activities and organizational relationships

Unlike the almost godlike qualities often attributed to leaders, there is no magic here. Exemplary followers are simply able to carry out their jobs and to work with others in a way that adds considerable value to the enterprise. It is how they go about these tasks that makes them stand out from other followers.

This chapter and the next will focus on the job and organizational skills necessary for exemplary followership. The following two chapters examine the moral dimension that underlies the followership role.

How Exemplary Followers
Add Value Through Their Jobs

The first hurdle facing followers is to demonstrate their value. Leaders and co-workers alike want to know what you can bring that will help the organization achieve its goals. Followers are expected to prove themselves. The first testing ground is usually the job itself. People want to see if you can do the jobs given to you and at what level of competence.

Your fate as a follower, then, is determined in great part by how you carry out your job. If you do not pass this first hurdle, you will generally not be prized, let alone given opportunity to use other valuable skills you might possess. You will be left out of key meetings and important networks. Your potential effectiveness will be blunted.

What separates an exemplary follower from someone who does really good work is the notion of "value added." For instance, some people do an excellent job, but on work that never should have been done in the first place. Much bureaucratic busywork falls into this category. Likewise, the owner of a maid service explained how two equally skilled and hardworking maids received quite different reviews from customers. One asked the customers what mattered to them and did a thorough job in those areas. The other had her own checklist that she followed. The customers raved about the former, while the latter drew mixed reviews. One customer complained that the latter maid spent an hour making the stove spotless. But the stove was relatively clean to start with and, from the customer's perspective, didn't need additional cleaning.

Adding value, then, goes beyond doing a good job. It means making a positive difference in accelerating the organization toward its goals. Followers who make more of a difference add greater value. An editor whose books increase the publisher's reputation and market share, not just profitability, adds more value than an editor whose books contribute profit only.

Adding value is the refrain of exemplary followers. They accomplish it by:

- Focusing on the goal.
- Doing a great job on critical-path activities related to the goal.
- Taking the initiative to increase their value to the organization.
- Realizing they add value not just by going above and beyond their work but in being who they are—their experiences, ideals, dreams.

This last is especially important. Japanese samurai were excellent followers of great generals. They learned not only the art of war but also the art of poetry, because a developed character was essential to the tough work they faced. They could not simply be killing machines.

Exemplary followers structure their work and carry out their day-to-day activities to maximize the human value added. Let's take a closer look at how they accomplish these.

131

Focus and Commitment

Exemplary followers are purposefully committed to something—a cause, a product, an organization, an idea, a person—in addition to the care of their own lives and careers. For some, this commitment is a passion that engages their hearts as well as their minds, emotionally fueling their everyday work activities.

Many exemplary followers come to the organization with a predetermined purpose to achieve through the organization. One medical researcher told me that she wanted to eradicate diabetes. She chose this goal as a result of watching her mother struggle with the disease for twenty years before succumbing to it.

However, this is more than choosing a career. It's more than asking, "What kind of work do I want to do?" and concluding, "I like to work with people, therefore I'll become a social worker." That is how people find jobs, but it is not enough for becoming an exemplary follower. Instead the best go a few steps further by asking, "What do I want to achieve? What will I commit myself to? What organizational vehicles exist for channeling my energies?" After all, how can you be an exemplary follower if you don't know what it is you are following? Armed with a personal dream, exemplary followers seek out organizations that are aligned with their own sense of purpose.

When following, however, most people are not so goal-focused. They are usually content to let the leader pick the goal and then carry out their assignments. While doing so, they try to maximize their personal goals, such as gaining work experience, getting ahead, or simply putting in eight hours of work for eight hours of pay.

To add more value, become more goal-focused. First, identify what you want to commit yourself to. For some people, like the diabetes researcher, this decision is driven by early life experience. Others come to it later in life after knocking around a bit, trying to find their niche. A grade school English teacher had been an actor, waiter, and telemarketer before deciding on his current career. His interest grew out of a conversation with his five nephews and nieces, aged seven to twelve. Their poor language abilities shocked him enough to send him back to the university for training as a teacher.

Finding your passion in life is a very personal journey. We all approach it in our own way and our own time. I only know that it is a common characteristic of exemplary followers. The power of goals clearly makes a difference. Success starts with a concrete commitment. Surprisingly, few people make that commitment.

In 1953, the graduating class at Yale University was surveyed. Three of the twenty questions asked about goals:

- Have you set goals?
- Have you written them down?
- Do you have a plan to accomplish them?

Only 3 percent of the class marked "yes" for all three questions.

The surviving members of the class were surveyed in 1973, twenty years later. The 3 percent who'd said "yes" concerning goals were more successful, had better health, and reported a happier family life. Strikingly, this 3 percent possessed 97 percent of the net worth of the class of '53.

Exemplary followers are like those 3 percent. They possess 97 percent of added value and goal accomplishment. They are more likely to see their dreams come true—to attain what motivated their following—because they have clearly specified it. This purposeful commitment gives them a distinct advantage over other followers in achieving success. Also, the leader will view them as more attuned to the organization's goals. This positive perception enhances their position and ability to add value.

The environments that bring out the best in followers are those where the goals are shared by the followers. The medical researcher I mentioned works in a top-notch diabetes research lab. Likewise, a grammar school committed to language arts hired the English teacher. The synergy in these matches is obvious and real.

Companies without a clear identity, vision, or product have a harder time developing good followers. Followers in these organizations muddle around trying to figure out what the company stands for or what it does. As one employee at FMC said, "What is an FMC?" Since their followers do not know if the organization's goals are aligned with their own personal dreams, these companies lose both the synergy and the enthusiasm that followers might bring. These companies inadvertently condemn themselves to mediocre followership.

Likewise, many people, especially young graduates just starting out, do not bring the benefits of such synergy. Chances are they haven't identified their long-term commitments yet; nor have they thought about how their goals and the organization's goals mesh. For their own part, they feel lucky to have a job where they might get some experience to parlay into a better job.

You diminish your potential value to an organization if you are not attuned to its goals. If you don't bring your own commitment, then the alternative approach is first to find out what the organization's goals are. Through this process, you might discover something that you can get solidly behind. Perhaps it won't be the same as the diabetes researcher, but it may be enough to get you excited about your work and give you a more noble purpose for coming to work each day than just picking up a paycheck.

Exemplary followers see clearly how their jobs relate to the larger enterprise. Gather background information about the company, such as the annual report distributed to shareholders and reports filed with the SEC. Learn who the company's customers are and how the company makes money from those customers. Go to a library and run a literature search about your company. From this background reading, try to determine the company's stated goals, its strengths and weaknesses, where it is doing well, and where it is feeling pain.

If they are available, read the mission and strategy documents related to your work group. Study closely the short- and long-term targets, especially the measures that will be used to determine if the targets are reached. Are the goals stated in sales revenues, cost savings, productivity improvements, or something else? These measures are important because they eliminate the platitudes and tell you what the real goals are. The measures are what everyone will focus on at evaluation time.

How do your department's goals on paper compare

with the goals of the larger organization? Are they in sync or in conflict? Have some important corporate goals been overlooked by your department? This comparison will help you see how closely linked your department is with the larger organization.

With this background, you are ready to figure out the goals of your division and department. See if what seems like an obvious goal from the outside matches the internal view. This is not always the case. Recall David Newell's observation about the values and goals of the television program *Mister Rogers' Neighborhood*. A new employee might conclude that the organization is in the television business and devote effort to that end. But the real goal is to help children and families grow. TV is simply the medium. To succeed, workers must focus on the child development goal first and television as a means to reach the goal second.

Start with the best one or two co-workers in the department. Take them to lunch or stop by their office at a convenient time. Ask them what the department's goals are. Which are most important? How does the work of your department fit into the work of the entire organization? How does it jibe with interfacing work groups?

Next, talk with your boss. Explain that you want to be in sync with her or his efforts. To do so, you need some straight, firsthand information. Ask him or her the goals for your department and what their relative importance is. Inquire about problems that will constrain your department from reaching those goals. How do your department's goals fit into the goals of the next-larger organizational unit? Where is the department headed over the next three to five years? Find out who the customers are for your department's work and how satisfied or dissatisfied they are. How is your specific assignment tied into all this? Is there something more you can do to help achieve your boss's goals for the department? How could you personally improve?

Ask your boss if you might repeat the interview with his or her boss. Explain that your goal is simply to understand the bigger picture so that you can be the best follower possible. Be sensitive to your boss's reaction. Some will give you the go-ahead, while others might think it politically incorrect. If your boss falls into the latter category, then back off gracefully. You will then have to use departmental meetings where your boss's boss is present to learn about his or her views on the bigger picture.

Finally, go talk to some customers of your department's work, as well as those paying customers who buy the product or service that your department contributes to. What are their expectations for and delight with the work product's performance, cost, ease of use, innovativeness? Do your customers like dealing with your department or do they see you as a pain? Do they give unsolicited positive recommendations of you and your work product to others? If not, what will it take to make this happen?

As a result of this process, you should have a clear grasp of where your organization is headed and how you fit in. Hopefully, you will have found a goal or two that you can work toward with enthusiasm. Perhaps you uncovered a blind spot between your department's goals and your customer's expectations. This blind spot may very well be a job you want to tackle. Or you might discover that you are in a department that doesn't suit you, but that another part of the company is doing work that excites you. With this information, you can now start to get yourself there.

The important point is to find something you care about, some purposeful commitment that will guide your involvements, keep up your spirits during the drudge work, and stimulate you to push the limit of your own performance.

The organizational opportunities created by this kind of commitment are clear. On the one hand, commitment is contagious. Most people like working with colleagues whose hearts are in their work. Morale stays high. Workers who begin to wander from their purpose are jostled back into line. Projects stay on track and on time. In addition, an appreciation of commitment and the way it works can give leaders an extra tool with which to understand and channel the energies and loyalties of their subordinates.

I remember observing a team of investment bankers putting together an employee-owned leveraged buyout. Working around the clock on the deal to meet the deadlines, most of the team members were initially motivated by the fees to be made. Yet one of them kept talking about the thrill of helping make corporate democracy a reality. In her mind, they were making history happen. Pretty soon, the others were talking about it. A higher cause had lit their fuse. Suddenly, they were fired up, doing a better job.

Competence in Critical Path Activities

Exemplary followers do a great job at tasks important to the organization. In his book *Flow: The Psychology of*

Optimal Experience, Mihaly Czikszentmihalyi describes Joe Kramer, a welder in a South Chicago plant where railroad cars were assembled. Joe worked for over thirty years in the plant and declined several promotions. He claimed that he liked being a simple welder and felt uncomfortable being anyone's boss.

Although he stood on the lowest rung of the hierarchy in the plant, everyone knew Joe, and everyone agreed that he was the most important person in the entire factory. The manager stated that if he had five more people like Joe, his plant would be the most efficient in the business. His fellow workers said that without Joe they might as well shut down the shop right now.

The reason for his fame was simple: Joe had apparently mastered every phase of the plant's operation, and he was now able to take anyone's place if the necessity arose. Moreover, he could fix any broken-down piece of machinery, ranging from huge mechanical cranes to tiny electronic monitors. But what astounded people most was that Joe not only could perform these tasks, but actually enjoyed it when he was called upon to do them.

Once exemplary followers are committed to an important organizational goal, they put themselves on the critical path toward its accomplishment. They find out what the "bottom line" is for the goal—that is, how will it be measured and who will do the measuring? They then figure out all the work steps involved in achieving the goal. Finally, they make sure they are part of those critical work steps rather than on the periphery.

This is all easier, of course, if the work you do is at the heart of the organization. Each company has its own critical path which is tied to the making and selling of its products or services. In a proprietary-drug company like Merck, the critical path starts in research and development, which invents the new drugs that are the lifeline to its mission and profits. In a generic-drug company that copies other firms' R&D efforts, the critical path is low-cost manufacturing and sales.

If you are an accountant, then, you generally are better off working for an accounting firm than for another kind of company. At an accounting firm, you are doing *the* work of the enterprise. You are bringing in the customers and earning the revenues. You are a first-class citizen.

In a plastics-manufacturing company, accountants are not usually viewed as on the critical path. Instead, others see them as a necessary evil, imposed by the government, or bean counters who make everyone's life miserable. Since they are not seen as contributing to the bottom line, they are labeled an overhead expense, which the production people grumble about paying for. Accountants in this case might feel like second-class citizens.

If you have a choice, then, go with a company where your work is directly on the critical path of the most important goals. You will improve the odds that your followership contributions add important value.

But many people are not in that fortunate position. Instead, they are like the accountant in the plastics firm. Even these followers can become exemplary by taking certain steps to add value.

First, link the bottom-line company goals to the

work of your department. Let's say the plastics company has three goals: to be the leading manufacturer of human prosthetic devices, to use more recycled plastic in manufacturing, and to increase profits by 15 percent per year.

Many staff accountants would see little connection between their work and these company goals. An exemplary follower would see several. To be a leading manufacturer means having timely and accurate cost data for you and your competitors. The accounting staff could provide this information. It can also mean reducing costs. The accounting departments could pinpoint where costs are high and propose changes. If production costs are high due to small batch orders, then a different production schedule might be in order. The accounting staff also might figure out ways to reduce the costs of its department, thus adding to the increase in profits.

Second, after linking your department's goals to the company's, translate them into actual work steps for you:

- Identify activities that contribute to the critical path.
- Determine the work skills you will need.
- Set a work schedule.
- Do the work that adds value.
- Measure your value added.

Exemplary followers make a habit of asking themselves, "Is the task I'm getting ready to do on the critical path?" The goal and its critical path become standards against which work activities are compared. Whenever they face a choice between two activities, they lean toward the critical path. This gives them tremendous focus so that they don't get sidetracked.

Commitment and focus are not enough, however. You must be competent at what you do. Dedicated incompetence is still incompetence. Exemplary followers distinguish themselves by mastering skills that make them indispensable to their organizations. By knowing what the company, department, and leader are trying to achieve, you can determine what essential skills will help them the most. Then build a distinctive competence that sets you apart from other co-workers and makes you more valuable.

Often this is done by searching for overlooked problems. One woman I interviewed described her efforts to build a competence that compensated for a dangerous blind spot at Alcoa, the company she cared about. Young managerial talent in this manufacturing corporation usually made careers in production, as this was the traditional route to the top. She asked herself how she could add value to the company by filling a critical void. Convinced that foreign competition would alter the shape of the industry, she realized that marketing was a neglected area. She took classes, attended seminars, and read widely. More important, she visited customers to get feedback about her company's and its competitors' products, and she soon knew more about the products' customer appeal and market position than any of her peers. The extra competence distinguished her from the crowd of production mavens and did wonders for her own career. Just as important, it also helped her company weather a storm it had not seen coming.

After you know what work must be done and you have the skills to do it, set a work schedule. Lay out a plan with due dates. Since most people cannot wait long periods of time for a sense of completion, break bigger projects into smaller sub-projects. This psychological trick makes the light at the end of the tunnel seem closer.

If need be, talk to your boss or other colleagues who are good at scheduling. At a minimum, ask them to review your plan to make sure you haven't left out something essential and that your dates are realistic.

As a result, you should have a list of prioritized sub-goals. Each sub-goal should have a due date, a review date before the due date to check the work product's acceptability, and a "to do" list of activities that will result in sub-goal completion.

Exemplary followers review their progress daily and/or weekly. If a snag or crisis hits, they reorganize priorities. To limit surprises, they keep key people informed of their progress rather than wait for those people to initiate it. This can be a brief memo or a short face-to-face meeting. They also analyze their own performance, figuring out ways to become more productive and to make the work more fun. They observe or ask others for input.

Effective followers also determine early and accurately the criteria for success in the environment, distinguishing between the apparent criteria and those that really count. They demonstrate their competence through concrete focused contributions which build a quick track record of successes in tasks that are important to the leader and the group. Rather than the big-bang achievement that takes a long time to pull off, they seize smaller victories that accumulate into a "can do" aura.

For example, two fund raisers received very different reviews from their co-workers and leader. One went after the big money by choice, hoping to snare a few sizable donations and be the hero. After three months, she was still wining and dining potential donors but with no pledges or cash to her credit. Her counterpart pulled in a string of donations ranging from $5,000 to $20,000. At the end of six months, the big-game hunter finally cornered one donation for $125,000. In the meantime, the other fund raiser had brought in a steady number of donations raising her total to $140,000. Although the total dollars for each were very close at the end of six months, the big-game hunter's catch was anticlimactic. Since she had not established credibility in the preceding five months, her success was attributed to luck. Meanwhile, her "small victories" counterpart was viewed as an extremely credible fund raiser. During staff meetings to discuss campaign strategy, the latter's views were listened to, while the former's were dismissed as infeasible or unrealistic.

Whether striving for better performance, higher profits, lower costs, improved quality, or faster production, exemplary followers track and document the value they add. This measurement has two functions. On the one hand, it yields the raw data you need to do a better job the next time. On the other hand, it demonstrates how you contributed to the leader's and the organization's goals. It shows that you are part of the team trying to make the goal a reality.

My research also revealed that exemplary followers make a point of doing a superb job of adding value through their core responsibilities before they tackle any additional responsibilities. Activities outside of your job description are luxuries which are best indulged in only after you do well what you are paid for.

One study participant described the risks of being diverted. A co-worker in the MIS department volunteered for several task forces that were not part of his job description, including affirmative action, United Way, and software standards. Arriving early and working late, he often took on special assignments for these task forces. However, he continually missed deadlines for producing reports that were part of his job description responsibility. Since other members of the company depended on those reports, they began complaining to his boss, who in turn gave him a low performance evaluation. This shocked him, especially since he expected kudos for all his extra work. He learned an important lesson about followership.

Initiative in Increasing Your Value to the Organization

Once exemplary followers have their assignments under control, they don't just sit back. If they have the time, they look for other activities related to the critical path. These generally fall into three categories:

- Developing additional expertise
- Increasing their scope of critical path activities
- Championing new ideas

The best followers think about what might make them a more valuable asset to co-workers and the leader. Like the previous example of the production manager at Alcoa who learned marketing, identify where the knowledge gaps are along the critical path and try to fill them. Or acquire knowledge that makes you a valued resource to your colleagues or the leader.

145

You might even offer to teach a course in it or mentor others.

Exemplary followers prevent professional obsolescence from sabotaging career progress. Most career fields have an increasingly short half-life. The responsibility to maintain leading-edge skills is yours, not the organization's. If you depend on the organization or the leader for maintaining those skills, you will be sadly disappointed. Effective followers overcome professional obsolescence by investing in personal R&D. This means involving yourself in continuing education. Keep up with the "best practices" used in your industry. Get input from professional colleagues who work for different companies. Read outside your field. Attend professional conferences. Exemplary followers engage in these activities whether or not the organization supports, recognizes, or rewards these activities. This might mean taking the time and paying the expenses involved.

Less effective followers expect training and development to come to them. If the company will not pay for a seminar, they complain and refuse to pay the money. I have heard professionals say, "I'll be damned if I'm going to pay the fifty dollars for this journal if the company won't subsidize me for it." Without parental attention, their competencies depreciate. Then they act surprised when they are no longer valued.

Another way to add value is to increase the scope of your activities beyond your job assignment. Spot problems that are along the critical path. For example, at Federal Express, a clerk from quality control kept his eye on a function critically important to the company—billing. He noticed that some of the company's delivery people forgot to check the weight marked on the air bill against the actual weight of the package. This observation led to a series of changes that saved the company $2.1 million per year.

Once you identify a critical path problem, you can volunteer to fix it. One follower in a new product development team at AT&T discovered that no one was assigned responsibility for scheduling and coordinating the engineering, marketing, and manufacturing reviews for a new computer product. Rather than just pass this observation along to the team leader, this follower took the initiative and worked on the problem till it was solved. She worked out an interdepartmental review schedule, identifying who should be involved at which stage of development.

A final suggestion for adding value above and beyond your job is to champion new ideas. All too often, organizations get stuck in a rut, locked into the way things have always been done. They don't see how the world is changing. For example, the Swiss watchmakers ignored digital Japanese watches. When these companies woke up, digital watches were now a threat, not an opportunity. The best followers try to avoid such situations by scouting trends and new ideas.

If you have a new idea, think it through before you bring it to the attention of the leader and the group. Tie it to critical path goals. Document the costs and benefits. Test out the idea on others before making it public. If necessary, build a prototype. Once you are convinced it is feasible, then bring it up. Your chances of success are much greater at that point.

Then follow through with your idea. This doesn't mean you have to do all the work. It simply means that you assume ownership until there is a clear handoff to someone else.

7. How Followers

Weave a Web of

Relationships

High achievers—people who add value by doing a great job—pass the first hurdle of followership. But if that was all they did, they would be no more than great solo performers. Exemplary followership has an equally important organizational component. The best followers know how to get along with their co-workers and leaders in ways that benefit the organization.

Unlike followers who consistently try to maximize only their own self-interest, the best followers view the organization as a "commons." The term "commons" dates back to pre-industrial England. It refers to the pasture that townspeople shared in "common" with each other for grazing their livestock. The challenge facing the community was to enable everyone to feed their livestock without degrading the commons for future grazing. If one family maximized their feeding at the expense of the community, they gained in the short run. But if everyone followed suit, all the grass would get eaten, destroying the commons for everyone. For all to benefit, each family had to contribute to maintaining the commons by keeping their short-term selfishness in check.

The best followers treat the organization as a commons. Instead of taking a free ride at the organization's expense or focusing solely on their rights, they acknowledge the mutual responsibilities they have with others. Organizational life requires give-and-take if it is going to work. If you are going to drink from the organizational well, you must also help replenish it.

This attitude helps exemplary followers in their organizational relationships. Others do not see them as only trying to maximize their own self-interest. Instead, they are viewed as also being attuned to and keeping other people's interests in mind. This enables them to nurture and leverage a web of important social relationships that then further contribute to the organization's success. The three most important of these relationships are with:

- Teams
- Organizational networks
- Leaders

Building a Team of Individuals

The demands of the workplace are changing. As many bosses now have twenty to thirty people reporting to them rather than the traditional five to seven, followers can count on leaders less for direction or input. Followers must rely on each other more.

For example, in 1987, declining profitability and intensified competition for corporate clients forced a large commercial bank on the East Coast to reorganize its operations and cut its work force. Its most seasoned managers had to spend most of their time in the field working with corporate customers. Time and energies were stretched so thin that one department head decided he had no choice but to delegate the responsibility for reorganization to his staff people, who had recently had training in self-management.

Despite grave doubts, the department head set them up as a unit without a leader, responsible to one another and to the bank as a whole for writing their own job descriptions, designing a training program, determining criteria for performance evaluations, planning for operational needs, and helping to achieve overall organizational objectives.

They pulled it off. The bank's officers were delighted and frankly amazed that rank-and-file employees could assume so much responsibility so successfully. In fact, the department's capacity to control and direct itself virtually without leadership saved the organization months of turmoil. As the bank struggled to remain a major player in its region, valuable management time was freed up to put out other fires.

As this example illustrates, followers increasingly have to work with each other, and teams are the most common vehicle for this joint effort. In the last ten to fifteen years, teams became ubiquitous. It is not unusual for the average worker to belong to several teams, many of which extend beyond their organizational unit. Most people alternate between team leader and team follower several times a day. These teams go by various names: leaderless groups, self-managed work groups, semi-autonomous units, task forces, committees, crisis units, SWAT teams, alliances, joint efforts, and councils. They all add up to the same message. The work of most organizations today is done through teams.

Exemplary followers, as we shall see, are good team players. But they also view teams with a critical eye. From their perspective, teams and the time-consuming meetings they spawn are often an inappropriate knee-jerk response to organizational challenges. Whenever an issue arises, some leaders react with "Let's form a task force to study the issue and have them report back to us." Teams, in some of these cases, are like the proverbial hammer that gets used for every job because it is the only tool in the box.

Before joining a team, then, exemplary followers ask whether the team is necessary at all. First, what is the task? Can it be written down in one or two sentences? Next, is the task itself related to the critical path? What is the likelihood that the outcomes will add value? Finally, if the task passes these two hurdles, is it something that is best handled by a team or by one or two people?

Once convinced that the task and a team are appropriate, exemplary followers question their own participation and that of others. What value do you and each member bring to this team? Are your talents suitable to the tasks? If not, are there better people to include on the team? Are all of you necessary or could you do with fewer members? If some people are on the team simply because they need to be kept informed or you need their political "buy-in," is there another way to achieve it without tying up their time and talents on this team?

Exemplary followers, then, are very particular about their team involvements. As one explained, "I view teams the way Charles Lindbergh viewed packing for his transatlantic flight. The plane would hold only a finite number of things. Excess items created more drag and required more fuel than the plane could carry. For each item he asked: Is this necessary to achieve the goal? I look at my team involvements the same way: Does my being on the team help me and the organization achieve our mutual goals?"

If exemplary followers don't buy into the team's purpose or goals, they share their views with the team leader up front, rather than be a noncontributing member. If they do join, they set about trying to make the team successful. Here in a nutshell is how they do it.

Start by checking to make sure that all the team members share a common understanding of the team's purpose and goals. Exemplary followers will often share their view and then solicit comments to either confirm or disconfirm their view. If team members are not on the same wavelength, keep pushing till a common understanding is reached.

Next, identify what your contribution to the team is and how it relates to the work of other team members. At each team meeting, commit to the timing and specifications of your output. If your work products are to be used by someone else, have them spell out for you what they expect. Then let them know what you can really deliver and when. Seek concurrence then, rather than down the line.

Exemplary followers try to maintain an equitable division of labor. This does not mean that everyone does the same amount of work. People's availability and talents will often dictate their contributions. Instead, it means not trying to weasel out of work at the expense of others and not letting someone else get saddled with more than she or he should have to handle. It also means chipping in to do your share of the grunt work, filling in for others when necessary, and helping to overcome bottlenecks in the team's progress.

After agreeing to your tasks, make sure you produce your work on schedule. If you are having trouble or getting behind on your schedule, let the other team members know as soon as possible, especially if they are depending on your work output. As one team leader explained, "If someone tells me of a problem before the due date, I view it as an acceptable reason. If someone tells me after the due date, I see it as an excuse." Try to show others your work before it is due so that you have time to act on any criticisms. If it turns out that your work doesn't meet the team's expectations, redo it as quickly as possible.

But team membership goes beyond doing your share of the work in a satisfactory manner. It also means helping out your teammates. As in basketball or hockey, this includes making "assists," where you don't do it yourself but you help someone else do it for the good of the team. The best followers gladly contribute by making assists because their focus is on the goal, not self-propulsion.

Willie Wise played forward on my college basketball team—a team that made it all the way to the NCAA semifinals. Willie was not the captain, the highest scorer, or the number one rebounder. He didn't make the most steals, nor was he the playmaker. The only thing that he led the team in was number of assists, setting up a teammate and then passing to him to make the basket. Willie was also the player who was always there when you needed him, whether it be for a pick, a pass, or a fast break.

After the season, Willie was overlooked in the pro draft. They chose the shooters, jumpers, and playmakers instead. Not discouraged, Willie tried out for the now defunct Salt Lake City team in the American Basketball Association. He not only made the cut, he became a starter. Again, he did not lead the team in anything except assists. What the team and coach found, however, was that Willie helped the team gel. He wasn't the leader, but he soon became critical and irreplaceable. His style of playing was the glue that held the "stars" on the team together. As a result, Willie made All-Pro year after year—a tribute to his contributions.

Likewise, exemplary followers are on the lookout for anything that might be useful to other team members. If relevant documents come across their desk or timely information buzzes in the grapevine, they share it. This is in sharp contrast to information hoarding, such as what once occurred at National Semiconductor. One participant described a manager there who received new and exciting results from a market research study he had commissioned. Upon reviewing it, he said, "This is great, but we can't let it leak out to those bastards. They'll try to use it against us." It turned out that he was not referring to competing companies but to the production people down the hall. Unlike this manager, effective followers realize that long-term success requires cooperation.

An important aspect of team membership is contributing to the team's dynamics. Besides coming to meetings prepared, the best followers try to help keep the team on track and all team members actively involved. Rather than focusing only on what you have to say, make sure that everyone gets a chance to speak and be listened to at team meetings. If someone's comments get ignored, point this out to the group so that the person doesn't give up and slide into passivity. If someone's body language suggests they are turned off or in mute disagreement, try to bring them back onto the team by soliciting their views. If you are personally frustrated with the group, others might feel the same way. Bring it up in a nonaccusatory manner to check if you are sensing a wider phenomenon. You might say, "I'm starting to feel frustrated because I think we're getting off track. Does anyone else feel this way?" By talking about it, you can help clear the air.

As part of the group dynamics, the best team players maintain a sense of humor and perspective. They help the team see the lighter side of the serious work. They are able to kid and be kidded, while being sensitive to others' feelings. But they also avoid being the class clown. Most importantly, they can laugh at their own mistakes and predicaments.

Finally, the best team players give credit where credit is due. They acknowledge other team members' contributions whenever they represent the team. If giving a presentation about the team's work, they start out by identifying everyone on the team. They use "we" rather than "I" unless they clearly did the work independently.

Building a Network

Teams and work departments exist within a mostly invisible stratum of organizational interrelationships. For lack of a better term, I refer to this as the organizational network. Networks include knowing the maintenance worker who can get you a hard-to-come-by table when you need one and a guru in another division who knows the ins and outs of the computer data base you are using on your project.

Your network is a series of interpersonal bridges that connect you to others in the organization. These connections seldom show up on formal organization charts. Nor are they heavily influenced by the organizational authority structure. People in your network do things for you because you have a relationship with them, not because their job requires it or the organizational chain commands it. You are much more likely to get a faster and better response from another department if someone over there is part of your network. This almost always beats talking to your boss, who talks to their boss, who then talks to that person.

Each person has his or her own unique network that branches in many directions. Networks crisscross over each other. This collective web of interrelationships is the real foundation of any successful organization. The traffic of organizational work travels over this invisible infrastructure.

Exemplary followers are sensitive to the role of organizational networks. More often than leaders, they see the effect of different decisions on the network itself. For example, executives may decide to reorganize a division because on paper it appears to be more efficient. Or they may decide to move from one building into two distant buildings to cut costs.

But exemplary followers are likely to see the ramifications of such decisions on the organizational network. The organization has an investment in the time and effort that followers expend to build their networks, let alone the benefits they produce. By moving people away from each other, the executives may destroy the very work relationships that are necessary for the organization to reach its goals.

Exemplary followers also strive to build a network because it is critical for personal and organizational goal accomplishment. To learn how, return to your critical path activities. Identify the key people in the organization who can help or hinder you in the completion of those activities. Then reverse the process. Whose work activities do you directly or indirectly help or hinder?

The people identified in both directions become the center of your network.

Now think further upstream and downstream from your immediate work. Once you hand off your work to someone else, who will help or hinder it in its contribution to the organization's goals? These people also need to become part of your network.

For example, if you work in R&D, you will probably need other R&D people in your network to give you technical input. But you will also want people in marketing who can give you customer input or put you directly in contact with customers. Likewise, you will need contacts in manufacturing who can keep you posted about factory floor changes that might influence your work.

When you are in meetings, observe who seems knowledgeable about topics important to you and who garners respect from others. Ask people in your department for names of people that you should get to know. Keep a list of the people who call you for information. All these people can be added to your network.

Once you identify the people, then you have to build the relationship. For some people, this is no more than introducing yourself and getting acquainted. Perhaps you share some hobby or have a common background.

But for networks to maintain themselves over the long run, they must be a two-way street. You must have something which the other party values. One good way to establish the relationship is to try to help them out *before* you need their help. Pass along articles or ideas that they have an interest in. Or maybe you have an expertise that they need access to. Perhaps you are a good listener or sounding board. Maybe your network is valuable to them, so that when they need to find something, they can call you for a referral. It could be as simple as being nice to them.

While building your network, pay attention to etiquette. Before you ask strangers for help, be sensitive to their needs and constraints. Ask if it is a good time to bother them. If not, choose a time and place that is convenient for them. So that you don't look like a lazy leech, never ask someone to solve a problem for you that you haven't first tried. Show them the process you used and the results. Pay attention to their answer, writing it down if need be, so that you don't have to bother them twice. If their help was considerable, let their and your bosses know about their contribution. Always give credit to those who help you. Finally, when it is your turn, reciprocate without hesitation.

Another aspect of etiquette is turf checking. Turf battles are much maligned in today's organization. But the best followers understand that people have both legitimate claims and vested interest in certain areas. If someone has spent five years building up an area, he or she expects to be consulted before people start reinventing the same wheel or tampering with it. The best followers will check with relevant people first and get their buy-in if possible. When there are overlapping interests, they will suggest collaborations.

Exemplary followers also collectively monitor the network for the "social loafers" who expect others to pick up their slack. People who try to get others to do their work or who try to get ahead at others' expense will often get a cold shoulder.

The power of networks, then, is enormous in accomplishing your job and helping the organization reach its goals. By cultivating their networks, exemplary followers increase their productivity and their effectiveness considerably.

Working with the Leader

The most important but troublesome relationship for many followers is with the leader. It can cause anxiety, confusion, frustration, and even anger. Conformist followers feel as if they always have to please the boss, while alienated followers continually snipe at the leader.

Effective followers see themselves—except in terms of line responsibility—as the equals of the leaders they follow. In the spirit of the "commons," effective followers take a barn-raising approach to working with the leader. In this era of distributed leadership, they realize that everyone takes turns leading and following. If they want the current leader to support them when the roles are reversed, they must be a fully contributing follower now. All too often, less effective followers do the minimum when following, saving their energy for when they lead. This results in team leaders who have to do all the work because their passive followers are focused only on their own leadership projects.

Exemplary followers begin by understanding the leader's needs, goals, and constraints. They make a point of asking the leader directly and watching where the leader puts his or her efforts. They also see that the people they follow are, in turn, following the lead of others. To the extent possible, they work hard to help their bosses achieve their own goals and the organization's goals.

Less effective followers, on the other hand, have a more limited worldview that only takes into account their specific work environment and immediate needs. They recognize their own work responsibilities and deadlines, but rarely consider the pressures and commitments their leader faces.

Exemplary followers work cooperatively with the leader rather than adversarially. They control their own ego to keep it from interfering with the leader's projects or other followers' effectiveness. For example, they distinguish between their own ego's stubborn preferences and an honest assessment of the ideas under discussion. When their ego is getting in the way of progress, they suppress it. Rather than always having to get their opinions heard, they help meetings move along in a crisp, productive fashion.

But when exemplary followers truly disagree on important issues, they are more apt to openly and unapologetically disagree with leadership and less likely to be intimidated by hierarchy and organizational structure. They do not accept the leader's viewpoint blindly. They make a habit of internally questioning the wisdom of the leader's decision rather than just doing what they are told. They assert their views even though this might produce conflict or reprisals from the leader. They especially speak out when they believe the leader is going down the wrong track or when the group secretly doesn't want to do what has been decided.

In many ways, followers are extended eyes and ears of the leader. They are often closer to the action and will pick up information that the leader doesn't have access to. Deprived of this information, the leader will make mistakes. Exemplary followers feel a responsibility to give leaders honest and candid feedback about their decisions and actions. They help the leader see both the upside potential and the downside risks of ideas or plans, playing the devil's advocate if need be. By disagreeing, exemplary followers help the leader do a better job.

When disagreeing with the leader, exemplary followers use these guidelines:

First, talk to the leader privately rather than unloading on him or her in a public forum. Avoid grandstanding, especially at the leader's expense. Instead, try to be sensitive to the leader's feelings and public image. Help the leader and other followers who might lose an argument to save face by pointing out the positives, as well as the negatives, of their viewpoint.

Next, pay attention to timing. If possible, don't approach the leader when she or he is dealing with a crisis or a deadline. Pick a time and a place that is convenient and without distraction. Disagreements that can hold till she or he is back from a trip or vacation will get a better hearing than those presented as the leader is rushing to the airport.

When you sit down with the leader, present the issue as a joint problem that needs to be discussed, not his or her stupid decision. State the issue clearly and succinctly from your viewpoint. Have your facts straight and at hand. One exemplary follower writes the issue down on paper and asks the leader to look at it. This helps to focus the issue and eliminate unnecessary confusion.

When presenting a problem, come prepared with

potential solutions. The boss seldom needs one more burden. If you are the kind of person who frequently dumps problems but no solutions, the leader is going to erect defenses against you. Not every situation, of course, lends itself to ready solutions. If not, at least do the legwork to find out the details of what is possible. Then at least you can suggest an approach to deal with it.

When brainstorming alternatives, consider your boss's point of view. Which alternatives might appeal to him or her? One exemplary follower queries herself, "If I were the boss, would I sign off on this and risk my reputation on its working?"—thus eliminating half-baked ideas. Whenever possible, offer alternative solutions in a form in which the leader only has to approve or disapprove. This saves the leader needless brainstorming and analysis.

Also, don't go in angry, because this usually induces anger in the boss. If you want the boss to focus on the merits of your argument, then work out your anger before the visit. Try not to let your bruised ego get in the way of your effectiveness.

Exemplary followers increase the odds that their voices will be heard by creating trust and avoiding the corrosive effects of mistrust. Likewise, they gauge how much they can trust their leader and their co-workers. Sizing up the leader's trustworthiness helps determine how they use their "power of the follower." In other words, they view credibility as a two-way street. They build it for others and demand that others build it with them.

Credibility grows with each action and day by day through consistent demonstration of trustworthiness. In my book *The Gold-Collar Worker,* I described how trust is built by making deposits in each other's emotional bank accounts. Deposits are made when you act responsibly, honestly, and caringly. A powerful emotional deposit is to help others get what they want. It communicates that you care about the person specifically. Extending yourself for another increases considerably the value of your emotional bank account and your credibility.

In Herman Wouk's *The Winds of War,* Pug Henry is a fictional naval officer who finds himself in the eye of major historical storms leading up to World War II. At one point, Pug and his wife, Rhoda, are invited to an intimate dinner party at the White House with President Roosevelt and a few other guests, including the British author and intelligence officer Somerset Maugham. During the conversation, Roosevelt asks Pug what he thinks of Hitler after having had a chance to talk at length face to face with him. After Pug gives his assessment, Rhoda blurts out:

> "Pug, when on earth did you have a talk with Hitler? That's news to me." The artless injured tone made the President laugh and laughter swept the table. She turned on Roosevelt. "Honestly, he's always been closemouthed, but to keep something like that from me!"
>
> "You didn't need to know," Pug said across the table.
>
> "Captain Henry," said Somerset Maugham, leaning forward, "I bow to a professional."
>
> The conversation broke into little amused colloquies. Roosevelt said to Rhoda Henry, "My dear,

you couldn't have paid your husband a handsomer compliment in public.''

Regardless of how you perceive Pug as a husband, his credibility as a follower who could keep confidences went sky-high. Honesty is a critical element of credibility building. Effective followers are honest with themselves, their co-workers, and the leader. When informing another, they tell the whole story, not just the part that makes them look good. They give credit where it is due and own up to their part in any mistakes. Less effective followers shade the truth, leaving others unsure as to what to believe.

Edward R. Murrow summed it up in the following way: "To be persuasive, we must be believable; to be believable, we must be credible; to be credible, we must be truthful.'' Credible followers, whose emotional bank accounts with their leaders and their co-workers are high, can make occasional withdrawals, such as missing a deadline, without doing irreparable damage. Others give them the benefit of the doubt. Less effective followers with low emotional bank accounts find their credibility extremely fragile. One false step and they may lose whatever credibility they had.

Putting It All Together

If you want to be an exemplary follower, you need to do a handful of very doable things quite well. The important points are to add value consistently in two ways:

- Do a great job on critical path activities.
- Nurture and leverage a web of organizational interrelationships.

The best followers are strong, independent partners with leaders. They think for themselves, self-direct their work, and hold up their end of the bargain. They continuously work at making themselves integral to the enterprise, honing their skills and focusing their contributions, and collaborating with their colleagues.

One interesting finding of my research is that exemplary followers don't believe they have to know everything. Instead, they actively learn by asking tons of questions, of the leader and their co-workers. They watch what happens around them. To them, followership is not an individual sport, like running a marathon. Instead, they get all the help they can without being a boor or a pest.

Hopefully this chapter has saved you some of that legwork by presenting some of what they have learned, the tricks of the trade that helped them become exemplary. If you still want to learn more, observe the best followers in your organization. If possible, ask them for advice.

Exemplary followership is not the exclusive domain of superheroes and demigods. Exemplary followers are ordinary people, not some idealized stereotype to be cloned. All of us are capable of doing the activities described in this chapter. The difference between the best followers and others is that the best actually *do* them. They echo Paderewski, the famous pianist. When asked by the Queen how often he practiced, he replied, "Every day." Impressed, the Queen queried, "Where did you get so much patience?" Paderewski pondered for a moment and then said, "I don't have any more patience than the next person. I simply use mine."

8. The Courageous

Conscience

Followers I've interviewed mention the moral component of their role more often than leaders do. I wondered why. I've discovered that followers face a difficult ethical situation vis-à-vis leaders. In having to follow others' decisions, the dictates of their conscience is overridden.

Exemplary followers handle this situation by exhibiting a unique attribute I call the courageous conscience. I define the courageous conscience as the ability to judge right from wrong and the fortitude to take affirmative steps toward what one believes is right. It involves both conviction and action, often in the face of strong societal pressures for followers to abstain from acting on their beliefs.

At some point as a follower, a leader may encourage you to do something you believe is wrong or to stop doing something you believe is good for the organization. Chances are the order will not be extreme; it will not jeopardize people's lives or constitute a gross legal violation where millions of dollars are at stake. Rather it will be something more ordinary, like altering a time sheet, withholding relevant information from another department in your company, padding a customer's bill, or producing products that have untested safety flaws. Or you may be working on a product to which you are personally committed and suddenly the boss orders you to "deep-six" it and reassigns you to something else.

When people talk about ethical conduct, they first think of one side of the ethical coin—that is, avoiding or correcting existing wrongs. But the courageous conscience goes beyond acknowledging and correcting wrong. The flip side motivates us to make positive contributions—for example, championing a new idea in the face of strong organizational apathy or resistance.

Pressures of Authority

What makes the follower's courageous conscience worthy of attention is the unique ethical situation in which followers find themselves. The leader-follower dynamic encourages followers to turn over decision making and ethics watching to the leader or the organization. They, not the followers, make the rules and establish the control systems for ethical compliance. Consequently, followers are often excluded from the ethical decision-making process. They are put into the position of being asked to do what someone else has decided should be done.

In their decision-making role, leaders generally contemplate a range of alternatives, weighing the effectiveness and ethics of each option. By the time the leader reaches a decision, she or he has deemed the level of morality acceptable.

Followers, on the other hand, are often presented the decision as a fait accompli. They are faced with a "yes-no" decision: do I do what the leader wants or not? Only occasionally are they party to the creation of options.

What complicates the followers' situation is that society expects them to trust and obey the authority structures—to make a moral leap of faith. Much of our social structure reinforces the leader's final authority and the follower's duty to obey. Religions teach us not to question God's laws or purpose. Obedience is explicitly codified in military law. When a coach tells you to run laps or a supervisor tells you to write a report, the immediate presumption is that you will do it. To obey is expected and rewarded; to disobey requires explanation and the risk of punishment.

The leader, then, benefits from the presumption of expertise, legitimacy, and trust, while followers have to overcome considerable social conventions to challenge the leader's position. Followers are understandably reluctant to do so, especially if it means questioning and raising judgments about areas that fall outside their area of expertise. What if they are wrong? What if the leader is right? If the setting were war, you could be shot for disobedience. If it were business, your career could be ruined if your faulty judgment disrupts the company's operations.

Challenging leaders also can be socially awkward. Confronting other people is seldom easy. After all, they didn't get in those positions without competence and societal backing. To question them is to question their credentials and the social order. It implies that you don't trust them, that you know more than they do, and that you are more important than the social order. This turns the social relationship topsy-turvy, causing fluster on both sides.

Given these societal pressures and norms, it is not surprising that many followers compromise their principles. As Stanford psychologist Phil Zimbardo points out: "Most people can be made to do almost anything if you put them in psychologically compelling situations, regardless of their morals, ethics, values, attitudes, beliefs, or personal convictions. People overestimate their power to resist external pressures, to take 'one little step' without being drawn into taking the final big step that may be alien to their natures or best interest."

These pressures clearly exist in the corporate environment. According to Bill Frederick from the University of Pittsburgh, 70 percent of the managers in one study reported that they felt organizational pressure to conform and often compromised personal principles. These ethical compromises occurred even though managers rate honesty, responsibility, and independence as the most important personal attributes, while placing obedience last on their list.

In one survey I distributed to 250 professionals and managers, 30 percent said they "often" or "always" accept what bosses, teachers, doctors, and other authority figures tell them without any questions. Thirty percent also agreed that when the leader asked them to do something that was not right for them, they usually did it anyway. After analyzing ten studies of ethical problems in business, Rick Wartzman of *The Wall Street Journal* concluded: "Even the most upright people are apt to become dishonest and unmindful of their civic responsibilities when placed in a typical corporate environment."

In addition, followers are likely to interpret top management's silence about ethical conduct as an indication that it is not important. For example, M. Cash Matthews, a Washington State University researcher, studied corporate codes of ethics. The vast majority only dealt with issues that directly affected the company's bottom line, such as conflicts of interest. Seventy-five percent failed to mention product safety, consumer relations, environmental safety, or the daily choices between right behavior and less than right (but not necessarily wrong) behavior. She concluded: "The codes are really dealing with infractions against the cor-

poration, rather than illegalities on behalf of the corporation."

In sum, then, followers face a unique and difficult
moral predicament. It leads many to do what they are
told rather than what they believe in. Yet a significant
minority do not cave in to the social pressure. Instead of
following orders, they follow their courageous conscience. From these exemplary followers, we can learn
how to stand firm in the face of social pressure.

Getting Your Courageous Conscience in Order

Many discussions of morality begin with the assumption that "I am good and I must protect myself from the
evil lurking out there." The courageous conscience
makes us aware that the struggle is first within us. Like
Cassius, it recognizes that "the fault, dear Brutus, is not
in our stars, but in ourselves."

In *War and Remembrance,* Herman Wouk has his
main character, the fictional World War II naval officer
named Pug Henry, translate the Wannsee Protocol during his retirement. This document is the contorted view
of what happened to the German Jews and why they
deserved it, written by an imprisoned German officer
while serving a sentence for war crimes. As an intro-
duction to the translation, Pug Henry writes:

> When I first submitted this article in translation to
> the U.S. Naval Institute Proceedings, the editor,
> Vice Admiral Turnbull C. "Buck" Fuller, USN, re-
> turned it with a large red-ink scrawl, *"Just what is*

*the purpose of offering to the Proceedings this ob-
tuse, cold-blooded, sickening drivel?"* He was an
old salt and a good friend. I wrote under his words,
"To show ourselves what we might be capable of,"
and sent the piece back. Six months later the article appeared in the Proceedings. I met Buck Fuller
on many occasions thereafter. He never once referred to the essay. He still has not.

In *People of the Lie,* M. Scott Peck ascribes the root
of most wrongs to either laziness or narcissism. While
there is some of both in all of us, my experience and
research teach me that followers are more likely to suffer from moral laziness, while leaders more often fall
prey to the grandiose self-infatuation that impairs moral
judgment.

Recall the two underlying dimensions of exemplary
followership: independent critical thinking and active
engagement. Whenever you are lazy in one of these,
you become less than exemplary. Nowhere is this more
true than with the courageous conscience.

Conformist followers who allow the leader to make
the moral decisions for which they are responsible and
who readily do what they are told are intellectually lazy.
Passive followers who act morally only under someone
else's prodding are lazy in motivation. Pragmatic followers who avert their eyes from wrongdoing rather than
stop it or who are unwilling to disturb the status quo to
do something worthwhile that needs being done are
lazy in action. In sum, we are lazy when we fail to make
necessary moral judgments and take the necessary
steps.

Followers can also become lazy about their own

attitudes, letting their egos get out of control. Convinced of their own superiority, some alienated followers cannot tolerate criticism of their ideas or performance. Their self-centeredness blinds them to the perspective of others. Some pragmatic followers believe it is okay for the larger group to be inconvenienced or suffer in order for them to get what they want. These followers are morally lazy when they equate right with what serves their interest.

Exemplary followers protect themselves from moral laziness by first recognizing how easy it is to become lazy. Most followers do not lose their conscience over extreme situations, like being ordered to intentionally harm someone. These situations are too rare. Instead, we are lazy for more mundane reasons—neglect, exhaustion, boredom, or lack of respect. We go to work, send the kids to school, clean house, fix dinner, or watch TV. While doing the best we can to lead our lives, it is sometimes simply easier to let the moral side slide. Raising a fuss only adds more work and anxiety, one more thing to deal with in an already over-scheduled life.

Exemplary followers must be vigilant about moral laziness. It is neither easy nor a one-shot effort. In this respect, we are wise to listen to Confucius:

> The ancients who wished to demonstrate illustrious virtue throughout the Empire first ordered well their own states. Wishing to order well their own states, they first regulated their families. Wishing to regulate their families, they first cultivated their persons. Wishing to cultivate their persons, they first rectified their hearts. Wishing to rectify their

hearts, they first sought to be sincere in their thoughts. Wishing to be sincere in their thoughts, they first extended to the utmost their knowledge. Such extension of knowledge lay in the investigation of things.

Duty to Disobey and Duty to Take Positive Action

Unlike leaders, whose ethical dilemma is in sorting out the options to make a decision, followers face the unique dilemma of obeying, not obeying, or taking alternative positive action. The followers who give in to the pressure of authority even when it goes against their better judgment focus primarily on their "duty to obey." Exemplary followers, on the other hand, realize they have a corresponding "duty to disobey" when appropriate to protect the organization and even the person who may be unknowingly ordering that a wrong be committed. In other cases, there is an additional duty— that is, to take action that leads to a positive contribution.

For example, in 1974, Art Fry had a new product idea for 3M. The marketing division told him customers didn't want it. Manufacturing told him the product was impossible to make. Although Bob Molenda, his boss, liked the idea, he had been told to assign Fry to another project. But Fry and Molenda didn't cave in and just follow orders. Instead they pursued what they believed was best for 3M. Together, they turned around the naysayers, slowly convincing them that the product not only could work but could also be one of 3M's biggest products ever. The resulting Post-It notepads became 3M's hottest product in decades, winning customer and industry accolades.

The exemplary follower recognizes that the traditional authority structure has a positive and a negative side. This social convention built the pyramids, won World War II, and made many a championship team. At the same time, it led to universities and defense contractors overcharging the government, allowed synthetic chemicals to be passed off as apple juice to unsuspecting babies, and resulted in a faulty O-ring which destroyed the space shuttle *Challenger*.

The courageous conscience helps us distinguish among our duty to obey, our duty to disobey, and our duty to take positive action. It helps us avoid what social ethicists Herbert Kelman and Lee Hamilton refer to as "crimes of obedience." Our society discourages disobedience and labels as criminals those who disobey legal authority. Yet Kelman and Hamilton argue that it is sometimes criminal to obey and that these crimes are more insidious. They occur when individuals forsake personal responsibility for actions they take under superior orders but which are considered illegal or immoral by the larger community. They are the consequence of overdeference to authority, when people continue to obey even though they should disobey or take an alternative action toward what they believe is right.

But when do you exercise these alternative duties? Unlike the alienated follower who is constantly at odds with the authority structure, exemplary followers choose their battles wisely. They ask themselves these six questions.

1. What is at stake for the organization?

Decisions or orders that deserve scrutiny are those that place the goal or the organization at an unnecessary ethical, financial, or achievement risk. This goes beyond illegality to include orders that compromise the organization's reputation or the achievement of the overall goal. Decisions that divert resources from the goal or that fail to follow through with necessary actions can spark an exemplary follower's dissent. An aide to the mayor of Pittsburgh recounted how he challenged the mayor's decision to use scarce city funds on a summer boating festival when the mayor had pledged to improve lower-income housing. Likewise, decisions that undermine the organization's future health invite inquiry. Major U.S. banks could have used more exemplary followers who questioned the banks' decisions to make the risky real estate and South American loans that now threaten their financial health.

In determining what's at stake, exemplary followers check themselves to make sure they are simply not sore losers protecting their own pet projects. The issue must go beyond their own self-interest to include protecting the organization's interest.

2. What will happen if you fail to act?

Many people feel justified if they do not participate actively in wrongdoing. If the boss is altering time cards and orders them to do so, they have a clear conscience if they do not obey. Pragmatic followers are likely to take a head-in-the-sand approach and hope it goes away. Yet the wrongdoing often continues.

Exemplary followers, on the other hand, feel a responsibility to stop the wrongdoing. They carefully weigh what can be done and how to go about it. As we shall see in the next chapter, this is no simple task. Choosing the appropriate channels that effectively end wrongdoing requires good judgment and some risk taking.

But once again, the exercise of the courageous conscience doesn't have to be dramatic. For most of us, the issue is less combating wrong and more the day-to-day courage it takes to make original, positive contributions to our organizations. Like Art Fry and the Post-It notepads at 3M, no intentional harm is at issue. Instead, it is that something positive will not occur unless we take action.

For example, when a Chicago citizens group organized a sports activities program for inner-city teenagers, their courageous conscience was at work. These citizens weren't combating an existing wrong. It is not illegal or immoral to *not* provide a sports program. However, the citizens who contributed their time and efforts helped these teenagers to grow in societally positive ways. It also prevented potential problems, since unsupervised teenagers with time on their hands are more likely to get in trouble.

3. Does the leader have both the expertise and the legitimate authority to issue this order?

Exemplary followers understand that almost everyone has a tendency to overreach now and then. Leaders often must make decisions under pressure and without complete information. If no one points out the technical or organizational flaws in a decision, then unforeseen and unwanted fallout can occur. In this way exemplary followers act as a check and balance on the leader's decisions. They can make sure that leaders act within their sphere of competence and utilize the best information available.

One red flag indicating that leaders are overreaching is when they cannot explain why the order is reasonable. Instead, their rationale is that orders are to be obeyed, implying that role obligations outweigh personal reasons or societal standards. If you ask for alternative justifications, such as knowledge or logic, and they are not forthcoming, then this should cue your courageous conscience.

4. Are human costs and societal values being overlooked?

Be wary when authority figures stereotype individuals because of their beliefs, role, or personal characteristics, as when the competition, the feds, Wall Street, or the Japanese take on the role of the enemy. Leaders who do this may be setting the stage to put aside accepted societal norms to discriminate against the targeted group. Being victorious becomes more important than how others are treated. This dehumanization attitude should signal that the situation may lead to questionable reasoning and outcomes.

For example, it was learned during the hearings on the space shuttle *Challenger* that the decision makers discounted the astronauts and their safety. It was as if they did not exist. As a result, other bureaucratic goals, like scheduling demands, overwhelmed concerns about safety.

5. What role are you being asked to play?

This question forces you to examine how close you are to questionable activity: what you know about it, if you have any reason to believe something is questionable, and how actively involved you are in carrying it out.

Exemplary followers are not ethics police in search of conspiracies to do wrong. The intent is not to go looking for problems, but to be alert when they happen under your nose or right next door.

Let's take a look at the Chrysler odometer case. In June 1987, a federal grand jury indicted Chrysler for selling sixty thousand cars and trucks during 1985 and 1986 as new when they had been used by Chrysler executives. In a routine practice followed since 1949, executives allegedly took cars off the assembly line and drove them around with the odometers disconnected. The odometers were then reconnected, the cars were shipped to dealers, and they were sold without a word to unsuspecting buyers. The indictment also charged that some cars had been damaged and were only superficially repaired. Once again, the buyers were told nothing.

In this case the mechanics who disconnected the odometers may have had little reason to question their orders. Odometers get disconnected for many legitimate purposes. The same is probably true for the people who repaired the damaged cars.

Yet the shipping, billing, and quality-control staffs were closer to the questionable activity. They probably had information that the cars were damaged but were being shipped as new. The managers who authorized disconnecting the odometers so that executives could use the cars were even closer to the wrongdoing. As you get closer to the potential wrongdoing and know (or should know) more, then your duty to disobey or take alternative action increases correspondingly.

Although most followers do not know the details of every operation, all of us have a general obligation to inquire into the overall purpose and reasoning behind the organization's mission and actions. It helps us to avoid unwitting crimes of obedience. For example, Scott Peck was stationed in Okinawa during the Vietnam War.

> I used to ask the troops on their way to battle in Vietnam what they knew about the war and its relationship to Vietnamese history. The enlisted men knew nothing. Ninety percent of the junior officers knew nothing. What little the senior officers and few junior officers did know was generally solely what they had been taught in the highly biased programs of their military schools. It was astounding. At least 95 percent of the men going off to risk their very lives did not even have the slightest knowledge of what the war was about. I also talked to Department of Defense civilians who directed the war and discovered a similar atrocious ignorance of Vietnamese history. The fact of the matter is that as a nation we did not even know why we were waging the war . . . we marched off to impose our will on the Vietnamese people by bloodshed with practically no idea of what was involved.

Despite all the flag waving and military parades surrounding the 1991 Gulf war against Iraq, one has to wonder if Scott Peck's analysis is still not as valid. Sure, Saddam Hussein is despicable. But were our followers, either in the military or at home, exemplary? How much did they know about Kuwait, Iraq, or the history of the region? Did we readily march into an unjust war?

6. What is at stake for you personally?

Exemplary followers are more likely to exercise their courageous conscience on matters of critical importance to their own value system. These are the issues that may cause them to resign rather than obey.

Exemplary followers have described three similar tests that help them identify issues and conduct that involve their personal integrity: the mirror test, the *New York Times* test, and the kids test. First, do they believe in their position enough so that they couldn't face themselves in the mirror unless they follow their conscience? Second, could they face their spouses, family, and friends if their actions are held up to the harsh light of public scrutiny, such as in the *Times?* Finally, if their kids were in their position, what would they want their kids to do? What would make them proud parents?

By tying self-esteem and personal principles to their actions, exemplary followers generate their own courage. The risk of external punishment is outweighed by the internal rewards of doing what is right and the risk of self-punishment for doing what is wrong.

These six questions can help you determine whether you have a duty to disobey the orders you receive or to take steps toward a positive contribution. They also highlight a key characteristic of followers with a courageous conscience. They try to be continually reflective, internally processing and evaluating what each order or decision means for the goal, the organization, and themselves. This does not mean they publicly confront the leader on every decision. When the leader issues legitimate and sound orders, the exemplary follower's internal evaluation is silently done. It only becomes heard when the duty to disobey or take alternative action is triggered.

But even when the leader is right, exemplary followers maintain their own independent thinking and critical judgment about what they will or will not do. They, not the leader, decide what role they will play and the significance of their actions.

As Thomas Jefferson said, "Eternal vigilance is the price of liberty." Followers must be morally on guard lest they become the unwitting victims of unchecked leaders.

9. Ten Steps

to a Courageous

Conscience

Assuming you decide to take a stand, the question then becomes how to do it. As discussed earlier, many social forces discourage followers from exercising their conscience. Most people will have self-doubts of one kind or another. No one wants to commit career suicide. Few people want to be seen as a troublemaker or, worse, a traitor. Simply questioning an authority figure can be embarrassing for all involved.

To pull it off requires a combination of organizational savvy and personal courage. If you go off half-cocked, use your ethics as a self-righteous sledgehammer, or turn purely personal disagreements into ethical sensationalism, you are likely to end up the loser without making any impact. Instead, you need to learn from exemplary followers who have succeeded. They use a combination of steps to confront leaders and to protect the organization, its goals, and themselves. But there are no guarantees. Not even the best followers win every battle. But by following the ten steps below, you can substantially increase the chance that your ethical stands will carry the day, and limit the fallout on your careers.

Again, you will notice that some of these ten steps can be used by anyone wishing to bring about organizational change. But they are particularly useful when followers question an order they believe is wrong or want to make a positive contribution in the face of status quo resistance.

1. Be proactive.

Exemplary followers do not see themselves as a moral adversary of leaders. They begin with the presumption that both desire ethical behavior and outcomes to occur. So rather than allow the situation to become a win-lose moral confrontation, they are proactive.

First, they realize that followers and leaders have different perspectives because of their relative position in the organizational structure. Exemplary followers appreciate that leaders often cannot see some ethical problems brewing simply because they are further removed from the front line. Or leaders might miss some downside ramifications of their decisions that followers can catch. Also, being more closely attuned to other followers, they can sense how their colleagues are reacting to the leader's decision or the situation. Given access to this information, leaders can often self-correct before going off an ethical cliff.

Exemplary followers also try to anticipate ethical problems before they occur. For example, if you think telling the truth is always important and lying is always wrong, then let the boss know before you are in a situation where the boss asks you to withhold information from a customer. Likewise, once a problem surfaces, nip it in the bud before it becomes a big problem.

2. Gather your facts.

Get your facts straight and make sure the leader has the same facts you do. If you can get agreement about the facts, you can sometimes snuff out a moral conflict in the making. What looks like a moral disagreement on the surface is often a disagreement about direction and potential risks.

Harvey Hornstein, a Columbia University business professor, studied over 200 managers regarding acts of courage in the workplace—everything from pursuing radically innovative product ideas to revamping nepotism-riddled hiring procedures. Almost nine out of ten of the managers who behaved courageously did so because of their belief in the strength of the facts.

This was clearly the case with Jerome LiCari, the

former R&D director at Beech-Nut. He long suspected that the apple concentrate Beech-Nut was buying from a new supplier at 20 percent below market price was adulterated. His department suggested switching suppliers, but top management at the financially strapped company put the burden of proof on R&D.

LiCari's staff conducted fresh studies to back up their claims. By 1981, LiCari had accumulated strong evidence of adulteration and issued a memo recommending a change of supplier. Yet most of the Beech-Nut executives took a head-in-the-sand attitude. According to one employee: "It was something you just hoped would go away." But LiCari was convinced that the supplies could jeopardize their new product line that emphasized nutritional value and the absence of artificial ingredients.

As Hornstein concluded about his courageous managers:

> For courageous managers, confidence in their expert ability and in their interpretation of the facts acted as a psychological glue binding self-identity to organizational performance. Consequently, when existing procedures and policies threatened incompetent organizational performance, it simultaneously threatened their positive self-identity. In order to preserve their identity and minimize internal, psychological costs, these managers had to express their opposition to the status quo and risk whatever external costs the organization might inflict.

3. Before taking a stand, seek wise counsel.
As in most things in life, it is smart to get a second

opinion—people who can help you interpret the facts and react to your proposed course of action. Pick someone—perhaps a mentor, former professor, or lawyer—who has the following characteristics:

- You trust them, especially their ability to keep confidences.
- They are knowledgeable about the pressures and perspective of the leader. This would suggest someone who is a current or former leader.
- They are savvy about organizational politics and protocol. If they know your particular organization, they are even better suited.
- They are willing to challenge your thinking and motivations, rather than simply agree with you.

You want someone who can see the situation from the leader's and your point of view. Legitimate alternative explanations might exist which you have overlooked. The world can look different when viewed from the power perch than it does from below.

Counsel need not always come from living people. When Admiral James Stockdale, the highest-ranking POW in Vietnam, returned to the United States, he introduced a course at the Naval War College entitled "Foundations of Moral Obligation." Through it, he tried to garner the moral lessons of authority relations learned from eight years of imprisonment. He found that

the single most important foundation is . . . history. That discipline gives perspective to the problems of the present and drives home the point that there is little new under the sun. Without familiarity with the yardstick of four thousand years of recorded history, busy people, particularly busy opportunists, have a tendency to view their dilemmas as unique and so unprecedented that they deserve to make exceptions to law, custom, or morality in their own favor to solve their problems. We can all think of several disastrous consequences of this shortsighted dodge within the last decade.

4. Build your fortitude.

The day-to-day courage required when you challenge the leader and take positive action is considerable. Says Hal Sperlich, who moved from Ford to Chrysler because of endless resistance to his idea for the minivan: "You're walking a very lonely road. Life in a large corporation is easier if you go with the flow . . . People who propose things that are different make more conservative people nervous, and the corporate environment just doesn't reward people for challenging the status quo."

The fortitude required by these "lonely roads" is not a God-given talent. It is something each of us must build up over time. Once developed, we must use it. If not, like any other skill, it will wither. This is especially true if the pressure is strong or the road is long.

Sam Snead, the legendary pro golfer, used an age-old trick against unwary opponents. Early in the match, whenever his opponent was on the green, he would give him the hole without the need for a putt. The opponent was generally glad to keep his score down and accepted the offer. Then, if the score was tight toward the end of the match, Snead would stop conceding the hole. Instead, he would make his opponent putt. In most cases the opponent flubbed it. He could not simultaneously deal with the pressure and perform after he had gone fifteen or more holes without ever having to putt. He was simply out of practice.

Courage also benefits from practice. When a friend of mine was in graduate school, she was afraid to speak to her professors. She didn't want to appear stupid in front of them or to challenge their authority. Yet she often found herself silently questioning their views. During her first year, she noticed that if she didn't speak up during the first class, she felt more anxious during the next class. If she had not spoken up by the third class, she was silent for the entire term.

Since she knew that advanced seminars would require her participation, she had to overcome her fear. At the start of her second year, she set new goals for herself. On the first day of class, she asked for clarification on the course requirements. During the second class, she asked a question about the course content. By the third class, she made an evaluative comment about the class readings.

In other words, my friend was practicing becoming brave. She didn't try to accomplish it all at once. Instead, she gradually built up her fortitude.

Any unskilled diver who has ever tried to dive off a high-dive platform knows how scary it is to stand three stories above the ground. Most who complete such a dive have worked their way up. They start with diving off the low board. They then move to a slightly higher level and get comfortable with the changes in motion and style. After four or five intermediate levels, they get to the top of the platform with the skill and confidence needed to execute a successful dive.

If you are not sure about how to stand up to authority, watch how other people successfully do it. Learn what works and model yourself after them.

To be prepared for the times of stress, integrate the skills you learn into your day-to-day relationship with the leader. Give yourself an emotional inoculation while the issues are noncritical. Initially, try disagreeing with the leader or the group over something small and inconsequential. For example, offer a different place for lunch the next time you go out. Once you are comfortable, move to higher-level disagreements, such as how to proceed on a project. Or challenge your minister on a questionable teaching of your religion. The goal is to obtain both the skill and the comfort level necessary to stop following altogether if need be.

5. Work within the system.
Most organizations have norms and protocol for airing disagreements. Exemplary followers find out what these are before taking any action. The protocol might begin by trying to work out the matter privately with the leader. Likewise, many organizations have ombudspeople or worker councils to whom you can voice concerns. Whatever the local custom, the important point is to demonstrate that you are working in a manner that is supported by organizational standards. It keeps you part of the community, rather than making you an outsider on the attack.

6. Frame your position so it will be heard.
Try to frame your position in terms consistent with the values and vision of the organization. You need to show how your position helps the organization get where it wants to go or how, by not heeding you, the organization becomes derailed.

For example, the first line of Johnson & Johnson's corporate credo reads: ''We believe our first responsibility is to the doctors, nurses, and patients, to mothers

191

and all others who use our products and services." As was widely publicized, when the Tylenol crisis hit, J&J followed their credo to protect the consumer. They recalled every bottle of Tylenol at a cost of $100 million.

A lesser-known story involves J&J's baby oil. In search of increased product revenues, J&J decided to market it as a suntan oil. While gearing up the advertising campaign, some followers got wind of the research findings linking suntans to cancer. Armed with the corporate credo, they successfully stopped the product's new marketing pitch, thus protecting J&J from accusations of insensitivity to consumer health. At the same time, they brainstormed other potential uses for the product. The end result was a new campaign to use baby oil for makeup removal—a safe and profitable alternative.

But not all companies respond to appeals to values. Sometimes you have to frame your position in terms of the bottom line. When Art Fry was developing Post-It notepads, executives at 3M put the project on hold for one month. He countered, "We can't do that, it will cost us a million dollars!" His rationale: "In a few years, we'll be selling more than a million dollars a month of these things. If we wait a month now, we'll miss one of those million-dollar months later." By linking the proposed delay to its long-term business consequence, Fry was able to get his project moving.

Columbia's Harvey Hornstein studied how organizations reacted when managers raised issues with different frames of reference. Managers differed in whether they linked their concerns to business priorities, ethical considerations, criticism of their boss's performance, or criticism of subordinates.

He found that by linking their concerns to business

priorities, managers maximized the potential for a positive organizational response. They even received promotions, perks, or other rewards for their efforts. In fact, 93 percent of all positive organizational responses to courageous acts occurred when managers used business priorities as a frame of reference. It also was most effective at minimizing the potential career costs to those managers.

In contrast, 42 percent of the concerns linked to ethics were either not heard or shot down. Criticizing a superior's performance fell on deaf ears. It also unleashed negative consequences, such as demotions or forced resignations, in one-third of the cases. Criticizing subordinates almost always produced nothing one way or the other.

When framing your concerns within business issues, Hornstein recommends focusing on solutions to persistent, nagging problems. Relieving the discomfort brings additional benefits above and beyond your idea's merits. It also gives you a step up on the nay-sayers.

For example, environmental activists were a thorn in McDonald's side. The fast-food giant spent considerable time and money combating them. A mid-level follower came up with the idea of co-opting them rather than fighting. He showed how it saved money, got the activists working for McDonald's, and put the company in the lead on environmentalism. His plan was accepted with overwhelming enthusiasm.

7. Educate others on how your view serves their best interests.

If you have done your homework, you have the facts at hand to back up your views. Prepare your position in a way that is concise and convincing. Chart the financial and organizational costs of the leader's order if it is carried out. Then show the benefits of your stand. Let the leader see why your view makes more sense from a purely objective standpoint.

Then turn to the subjective element. An old maxim goes: You can get anything you want in this world if it helps people get what they want. Nowhere is this truer than in follower-leader relationships. By combining your stand with what motivates the leader, you have a much better chance of being persuasive. If your boss is looking for a promotion, show how the order issued will interfere with that goal or might even lead to a demotion.

Your purpose is to convert the leader, not to intimidate. Leaders need to see that you are on their side, looking out for their best interests as well as the organization's. Thus, rather than just say no, which might threaten their authority and self-esteem, try to offer some feasible, nonthreatening alternatives to their decisions. Like the J&J baby oil example, these alternatives hopefully can realign the leader's objectives with the ethical guidelines of the organization or society.

In some cases, your intent is to motivate positive action, rather than stop wrongdoing. If you are pushing a new product idea, a prototype can help enormously. Seeing can often lead to believing.

In the late 1970s, a product-line manager in Tandy Corporation's marketing organization believed that personal computers could be a big hit in Radio Shack stores. His bosses nixed the idea. Personal computers were still more science fiction than fact. Undeterred, he built a prototype machine with the help of co-workers. When he presented his vision again, he had a working prototype on hand. With this physical demonstration, he broke Tandy executives out of their limited, status quo mind-set. As a result, Radio Shack became a major force in the personal computer marketplace.

8. Take collective action.

Sometimes one voice is simply too small. If like-minded people band together, then the chorus of voices can make the leader or organization take notice.

Collective action also reduces the anxiety experienced by followers when challenging the authority structure. In one computer company, many employees grumbled privately about the procedures for developing software. It wasn't until a group of them joined together to write a report detailing the problems that anything happened. They showed how it interfered with getting products to market faster and how it jacked up overall costs. Using a business focus and collective action, they succeeded in changing the system.

As peers share concerns via collective action, it also can reinforce a follower's own misgivings about the leader's orders. If the leader fails to respond, then it provides a supportive vehicle for massive disobedience. As the response of Soviet citizens to the attempted coup to oust Gorbachev demonstrates, entire groups can institute changes on a massive scale without the permission of higher-ups.

9. If you meet leader resistance, seek higher authority.

If all your good-faith actions prove fruitless, you may have to resort to higher authorities. This is a very risky action, since many organizations have strong norms against breaking the chain of command. Some higher-ups will back their subordinates even when they are wrong, simply to send a message that end runs are unacceptable for any reason. Thus, you need to know that this action can put your career at risk.

But not all companies are so hard-nosed. In fact, more and more are encouraging people to alert higher authority to organizational abuses. For example, a manager at Herman Miller fired an employee. Two other employees thought it unjustified and went directly to Max DePree, the CEO, with their complaint. He agreed to look into it. He spoke with the manager and others involved in the incident. His conclusion: the manager acted with gross unfairness. He reinstated the worker and fired the manager, who believed his authority should not be challenged. DePree's actions created an atmosphere where the courageous conscience comes before authority.

If the leader is the highest authority in the organization, then you might have to seek an outside societal authority such as government agencies, stockholders, or the press. Going outside the corporate family presents additional risks. Once again, you need to repeat your steps of choosing the right frame of reference, having the facts at hand, and using collective action.

Jerome LiCari, the R&D manager at Beech-Nut, did just that. He first went to his boss, the head of operations, who threatened to fire him. He then went to the president. When that produced no results, he quit, and contacted the FDA. In 1987, the company pleaded guilty to 215 felony counts of conspiracy to commit fraud by distributing adulterated apple juice. In 1988, the two executives were also found guilty on a majority of 350 charges.

10. Have the financial and emotional cushions to exercise other alternatives

It stands to reason that if you cannot pay for legal help or afford to lose your job, then you have more at risk. Legitimate whistle-blowers that I interviewed described the tremendous psychological and financial drain that resulted from their actions. Their courageous acts stigmatized them in the marketplace. As a result, all agreed they would still act courageously but would wait until they had new jobs lined up.

Financial resources can help cushion the negative fallout from your courageous acts. A friend of mine keeps a year's salary in savings as her "walk away" money. She wants to be able to leave her job and not have her family's standard of living affected, even if it takes a year to find a new one. This is her own insurance policy so that finances need not color her judgment.

Likewise, you should talk over your decision with family and friends who will support you during your time of stress. Talk about the potential consequences and what it means for them and for you. Have plans ready to deal with different scenarios, including what you will say to neighbors, co-workers, and, if need be, even the press.

"THE BRAVE CARVE OUT THEIR FORTUNE"

So Cervantes wrote in *Don Quixote.* Followers may suspend their right to make certain choices and vest much decision-making power in the leader. Yet exemplary followers know that freedom of choice has only been suspended, not surrendered. They maintain the right to determine whether the trust placed in the leader is justified by the quality of the leader's decision making and the outcomes of the leader's performance. Just as followers voluntarily vest power and authority, they maintain the right to divest and withdraw support.

By using the ten steps above to guide you to a courageous conscience, you greatly improve the odds of success. You act from a position of inner strength. In the final analysis, it is the striving for rightness, not just the outcome, which counts.

10. Leadership Secrets

from Exemplary Followers

You and I ought not to die before we have
explained ourselves to each other.

—John Adams to Thomas Jefferson,
September 10, 1816

Recently, Lee Iacocca
appeared on national television to discuss the contro-
versy over astronomical executive pay packages. His
defense of his multimillion compensation went like this:
"I saved Chrysler. I'm building brand-new cars. I'm
building new factories . . ."

If I were a Chrysler employee watching this spectacle, I wonder what my reaction would be. Would I be
proud of Iacocca and pleased with his personal identification with our company's work? Or, realizing that his
salary was a hundred times greater than mine, would I
resent that he was taking all the credit for our work?
Would I wonder when was the last time Lee Iacocca
drew a car design or turned a wrench on the assembly
line? Why didn't he give credit where credit was due?
Why didn't he say, *"We're* building a new car" or
"Chrysler employees are doing such and such"? Don't
we deserve some recognition?

I wonder if Iacocca considered the effect of his
statements on his followers. In today's flatter, leaner environment, organizations and leaders cannot succeed
without committed, contributing followers. You would
think that leaders would pay more attention to them.

But many leaders only look at the world from their
own or the organization's viewpoint. They are more
likely to consider how Wall Street will react than how
their own employees will interpret a decision or action.
Followers are only taken into account seriously when a
decision is so radical that it invites a mutiny.

Think of all the people in high leadership positions
in this country: top executives, religious leaders, heads
of civic organizations, elected politicians, and union
bosses. Add to these all the middle managers, ward
bosses, educators, and first-level supervisors. Then consider committee chairs and task force leaders.

Ask yourself: How many of these leaders and their
organizations achieve lackluster results because they
don't have the full support of their followers?

Leadership from the
Eye of the Follower

Based on my surveys, followers are very dissatisfied with the quality of business and government leadership in this country. From the followers' point of view:

- Two out of five bosses have questionable abilities to lead.
- Only one in seven leaders is someone that followers see as a potential role model to emulate.
- Less than half of the leaders are able to instill trust in subordinates.
- Nearly 40 percent have "ego" problems—are threatened by talented subordinates, have a need to act superior, do not share the limelight.

These statistics constitute a strong indictment by followers against the quality of leadership, and gives the lie to two current management gods: the god of "empowerment" and the god of "transformational" leadership, which supposedly remakes followers from a mindless mass into capable individuals. Whether the myth conjures up Gandhi mobilizing the masses or General Patton disciplining out-of-shape recruits into fighting soldiers, transformational leaders are lionized for bringing mightiness out of mediocrity. In this view, leaders are the active molders and followers are the passive clay. Influence runs in one direction only.

These statistics, however, tell a different story. Followers actively evaluate their leaders and find most of them wanting. Followers are insulted by the suggestion that they need empowering or transformation. They are not enslaved, waiting to be freed by benevolent masters. The major constraint upon their best performance is the stereotypes inside the leader's head.

Followers can be likened to customers "buying" the quality of leadership. They compare what one leader has to offer with other alternatives. Then they make their purchase.

In one large consumer goods company, a new division leader instituted a new plan along with a set of autocratic procedures to back it up. Within three months, 25 percent of the division had initiated internal transfers to other parts of the company. Two hundred followers in all did not "buy" the leadership being offered them and voted with their feet. Followership implies a voluntary choice, not a contractual one. Like volunteers, followers decide where to invest their time and effort.

What is it, then, that followers look for in leaders that will make them want to volunteer their best effort? I asked followers to answer that question by specifying what the leader actually does, day to day, for and with them. When followers answered with an attribute such as "honest," I pushed for what the leader did to demonstrate honesty.

My research reveals that, given the opportunity, followers would design their "model" leaders to:

- Embrace exemplary followers as partners or co-creators.
- Demonstrate the value they add to followers' productivity.

What follows is both a one-sided and a somewhat "ideal" model of leadership. It is one-sided because it derives only from the followers' perspective. It reveals what they want from leaders, recognizing that customers, stockholders, and the leader's own boss have equally valid claims on the leader. It is ideal because leaders like this don't exist . . . yet. Few leaders have seriously and continuously concerned themselves with the followers' perspective. Few role models exist. But they could, and if followers have their way, more will exist in the future.

Embrace Exemplary Followers as Partners or Co-creators

Exemplary followers do not want leaders who decide their work or their fate for them. They want leaders who view them as partners in shaping the enterprise.

In true partnerships, competent people join together to achieve what they could not achieve alone. Drawing from its legal definition, partnership requires the partners to be individually and collectively accountable for the actions and liabilities of the firm. Unless explicitly negotiated otherwise, partners are viewed as equals. As equals, they decide how to work together, to share power, and to reward individual and joint contributions so that the partnership succeeds.

Partnership Means Sharing Information

Because partners are accountable for each other's actions, they seek and share information. Too many leaders, however, hoard information—whether on budgets, key decisions, or financial returns. They view the dispensation of this information as a leader's prerogative. This approach generally breeds suspicion and resentment.

When Hugh Aaron's closely held plastics manufacturing company, called Customcolor, started losing money, he issued an austerity plan. Calling a company-wide meeting, he informed the employees that there would be no more overtime, bonuses, or new machinery. Wages were frozen. But the employees didn't believe the company was in trouble. They thought he was gouging them while keeping his own salary and perks.

To get the employees actively involved in turning the company around, Aaron reluctantly decided to show them the facts by opening up the books. Says Aaron, "Having built up my business through personal sacrifice and risk—from a money-losing operation into a prosperous, creditworthy enterprise—I found sharing its innermost secrets anathema, akin to revealing my sex life."

Although his accountant and business associates thought the idea was bizarre and dangerous, Aaron shut down the plant for an hour and held an all-employee meeting in the cafeteria. He went over the entire P&L statement, item by item. As it turned out, he had to hold several meetings to educate the employees in how to interpret the financial data. By sharing the bottom line and the details of expenses, however, he was also sharing the burden of having to take action.

The employees aggressively joined Aaron in reducing expenses. For example, not realizing that the company paid $16,000 each year for cleaning the workers' uniforms, they suggested that the company buy its own washer and dryer to shave expenses. The expense dropped to $4,000 per year—a savings equal to an office worker's annual wage. Likewise, they eliminated the Christmas party. Instead, they set aside and raffled off the accumulated earnings from the vending machines.

By sharing information, Aaron signaled that he wanted partners, not just employees. The employees responded in kind.

But sharing budget and financial performance data is only the first step in creating a partnership. Partners who are liable for each other's actions also share personal performance information. They touch base regularly to let each other know what and how they are doing, as well as to give feedback to each other.

For example, in a large computer company that I visited, managers held yearly performance evaluation meetings with their subordinates. The managers would discuss the subordinates' strengths and weaknesses along with goals for the next year. But they wouldn't reveal the actual 1 to 5 rating that they assigned to each employee or the person's rank compared with other employees. The company felt that the middle and lower performers would be demotivated if they knew this information. So the employees had to piece together cues from the manager's feedback. If they were told they were "solid and consistent," it meant they were a 3 or a 2, according to the employee grapevine.

The employees in this company did not know where they stood and they wasted much time trying to figure it out. In a partnership, people know where they stand. As equal adults, they don't need someone else to protect them from the reality of their own performance. Each is responsible for his or her own motivation.

While many performance evaluations focus on the

subordinate's leadership skills, it is important to devote a section to followership and partnership skills, including the ability to shift easily between roles. Evaluations can come from peers, customers, subordinates, and the person himself or herself. Anyone who comes into regular contact with the person being evaluated can complete brief periodic questionnaires.

The sharing is also a two-way street. Followers should evaluate the leader's performance. Upward feedback, as it is coming to be known, is essential for a partnership. Most leaders get very little direct feedback on their performance—partly because they don't ask and partly because followers fear the boss will retaliate. Although subordinate feedback can be threatening to your ego, who can better tell you what kind of leader you are than your subordinates?

If you want to solicit this information, emphasize that it is meant to help you become a better leader and that no one will be hurt for giving their direct, candid view. If trust is low, make it anonymous.

Don't ask general and vague questions, like the overall quality of communications skills. Instead, be very specific about behaviors relevant to the follower and the leader: "Do I return phone calls quickly?" "Do I listen with an open mind?" "Are we in contact on a daily basis?" "Do I make sure you understand before moving on to a new topic?"

Then ask each subordinate to rate the boss on every behavior and to indicate how important that aspect is to the subordinates in doing their jobs. Have space for subordinates to write in specific comments and what they would need to see from the leader to give a higher rating.

The leader can then share the tabulated findings

with the troops and tell them what she or he plans to do about weaknesses. This demonstrates to followers that they have been heard, allows them to help the leader interpret the findings, and enables them to contribute to the leader's development plan. It also gives them a chance to see if their individual appraisals of the leader match those of other followers.

Once performance data is shared, it opens the door to sharing an almost taboo topic—salary data. Many people are skeptical of sharing salary data. They believe it sets off a horse race, pitting co-worker against co-worker. But Ed Lawler's extensive research on open-pay systems consistently shows higher morale and trust in organizations that share this information. In the absence of valid information, most people's fantasies will fill in the vacuum with erroneous beliefs about how they are being victimized.

It is for these reasons that Steve Jobs, the CEO of Next Computers and the co-founder of Apple, posts every employee's salary, including his own. In this way, all employees know how they are valued relative to everyone else. As their contributions increase, they can see whether it is reflected in their salary standing.

Partners Co-create the Vision and Mission

Many leadership books tout the "visionary" role of leaders. Like Moses descending from the mountaintop, the leader unveils the new order. For their part in this scenario, dependent followers are supposed to stop wandering about aimlessly. Instead, they dutifully applaud, thank the leader profusely, and line up behind the leader's vision.

This scenario has little appeal to exemplary followers. They generally know where they are going. If not, they want to be part of the process that determines the end goal. This might be called "leadership by informed consent." As partners, followers want to forge the vision together to increase the probability of success.

To begin, the leader can present the first "straw model" so that followers can react, modify, and build upon it. For example, a CEO of a furniture company conducted twenty-six successive vision-building workshops with a different group of employees each weekend. The major purpose of each workshop was to build a cumulative vision for the company using the output of the previous session. Each successive group could challenge and change the previous output. The results of each session were published for everyone to see and comment on. At the end of the twenty-six weeks, a collective vision was established. Over the next six years, revenues soared from $6 million to over $70 million.

In contrast, when leaders develop a strategy without the help of followers, they are asking for trouble. A major money-center bank asked outside consultants to devise a new strategic plan. When top management unveiled to the bank's loan officers the new strategy of energy and Third World loans, these followers gave it a thumbs-down. These loan officers spend their entire careers analyzing strategic plans of companies seeking financing. They unanimously agreed that if their own bank asked for a loan on the basis of the new strategy, they would turn down the request. Rather than use this reaction to modify the strategy, top management shrugged off the criticism as due to the "Not Invented Here" syndrome and implemented the strategy. Consequently, many of the bank's top performers left rather than go down with what they called, and what eventually became, a sinking ship.

Partners Share the Risks and the Rewards

Exemplary followers are willing to put themselves on the line, but they believe their leaders should do the same. As Admiral James Stockdale said, leaders should only issue orders that "the issuer is willing to carry out by him- or herself in order to set an example." When the work is done and if things go well, all should share the rewards equitably. If things go poorly, all should carry their fair share of the sacrifices.

Some leaders say one thing but do another. Out one side of the mouth comes, "People are our most important asset." Out the other side comes, "Downsize and lay off." As Ilene Gochman of the Opinion Research Corp. of Chicago observed after her firm surveyed 100,000 employees: "Employees have seen that if the company steams off on some new strategic tack and it doesn't work, employees lose their jobs, not management."

Followers particularly resent the leaders' profiting at the followers' expense. The fact that the average CEO now makes more than a hundred times the average worker's pay does not escape their attention. Many followers would agree with Bud Crystal, a compensation expert and a professor at Berkeley's Haas School of Business "[CEO pay] may be financed from the bodies of middle management. By having leaner, meaner organizations with fewer levels, the CEO—on the seventh day he rested—takes half the savings and puts it in his pocket."

Followers increasingly carry the downside burden and gain little of the upside benefits. When General Motors' profit slid 13 percent in 1989, CEO Roger Smith's annual bonus fell only 7 percent to $1.4 million. Profit sharing paid to hourly and lower-level salaried workers plunged 81 percent to $50 a person. Likewise, the CEO of Firestone received a $5.6 million bonus for improving the company's financial condition. To accomplish that feat, over 50 percent of the work force suffered serious job disruption as the work force shrank from 110,000 to 53,500.

Today the odds are greater that many followers will be hurt before any leader is. If the company goes belly-up, most lower-level employees will have a much tougher time of it than a CEO with a golden parachute.

Exemplary followers prefer leaders who stand with them on the front line of adversity. Both Gandhi and Martin Luther King won follower support when they took the first blows from the police clubs. Jane Addams suffered severe social ridicule when she opened Hull-House to help impoverished immigrants in 1889. The personal sacrifice of these leaders encouraged their followers to overcome fear and to extend themselves for the greater good. Likewise, when Alexander the Great's soldiers were dying of thirst and starvation as they marched across the Indian desert, he walked with them to share their suffering. Alexander's personal sacrifices encouraged his followers to overcome fear and extend themselves for the greater good.

It is difficult to find leaders who would follow in Alexander's footsteps, but some do exist. And followers love them for not deserting them.

One such leader is Ken Iverson at Nucor, a minimill steel company with $1.1 billion in sales. Iverson built the company on sharing risks and rewards. He established a lavish but simple employee incentive system: the more steel produced, the more money earned by employees. The work force produces almost twice as much steel per worker-hour as its larger competitors. In a good year, Nucor employees can double their annual salaries.

The employees, however, carry more risk than their large competitor counterparts. If sales or productivity is off, they forgo the extra income. But even then Iverson takes the lead. When the company faced tough times in 1988, Iverson took the first pay cut, and at 60 percent, also the deepest. The end result is a much admired boss and a very profitable company whose employees' rave ratings consistently put it on the best-run companies lists.

Partners not only know how much the others make, they share the same pay formula. If the leader gets a 25 percent bonus based on increased productivity or sales, then subordinates would receive the same. One of the biggest demotivators for exemplary followers is a discrepancy between how they and the leader are rewarded. Why should a subordinate try to reach the goal if only the boss gets rewarded? If everyone stands to gain or lose proportionately, then a unified effort is more likely.

One manager at a wholesale company told her subordinates exactly how she was paid: 50 percent base salary, 40 percent on meeting sales goals, and 10 percent on meeting cost goals. She stood to gain a 10 percent bonus increment for every 10 percent she exceeded her sales and cost goals. Her annual take could realistically range from her base salary to 150 percent with bonuses. Previously, her ten subordinates were paid only a salary. She invited them to revamp their pay scheme to match hers. By accepting more risks, they increased the upside potential. Even though the boss's total dollar take was greater due to the larger base salary, they could make considerably more than their current salary.

The more risk-averse shied away from the offer, but six employees jumped at the chance. With their fortunes rising and falling in tandem, they now had greater motivation to work together and with the boss to meet the goals. In addition, no one could complain that anyone profited at the other team members' expense. For four years in a row, this team has been the top producer in the company. Also, the previously risk-averse employees have signed on.

Demonstrate the Value You Add to Followers' Productivity

Leaders traditionally believed that they added value to followers in two ways. First was being the expert on the follower's job. The leader could look over the employee's shoulder, give advice, and make sure the job got done right. This was a supervision-cum-development function. Second was to give approval and distribute the rewards for good work. Current business literature also suggests that the leader provides the vision and does some "transformation and empowerment" intended to jump-start the organization.

From the exemplary followers' viewpoint, however,

these functions are unnecessary. In many organizations, the followers know how to do their job better than the leader. This is especially true for technical fields where the actual job knowledge becomes obsolete quickly. The longer leaders are away from the technical job, the more dependent they become on the specialists working for them.

Likewise, exemplary followers look less to their bosses for approval. Bosses often do not have the expertise to determine the quality of the work itself. How could the boss give approval? Instead, these followers look to professional peers who can comment on the elegance and originality of their work. Also, as more workers get connected to either internal or external customers, they query those customers as to how happy they are with the work products. The boss, then, is simply left with deciding how much to pay or value the subordinates' work. But even that is being increasingly tied to concrete customer and profit targets on the front end.

The leader's vision, transformation, and empowerment roles also are superfluous for many exemplary followers. In fact, many would be insulted if leaders offered their vision as a fait accompli.

So what is a leader to do? What value can she or he add to exemplary followers? What will make an exemplary follower support one leader rather than sabotage or desert in favor of an alternative leader?

From the followers' viewpoint, leaders add value in two ways:

- Create environments where exemplary followers flourish.
- Be less a hero and more a hero maker.

Create Environments Where Exemplary Followers Flourish

This may involve many different activities, depending on the particular work environment. For example, it can be as basic as successfully selling the group's ideas and obtaining the necessary resources so the group can accomplish its goals. This may require representing the group to larger organizational units, including government or society at large. Even CEOs, like Ken Olson at Digital Equipment and Paul Allaine at Xerox, are spending more time assisting in the sales of their products to key customers. They view this selling as a critical part of their job and as a way to help out their followers.

Leaders also should remove roadblocks to a follower's productivity. They can shield the followers from the bureaucracy—the "administrivia" and minutiae that interfere with getting real work done. It is not unusual for large organizations to require many employees to spend 20 to 30 percent of their time filling out paperwork and preparing various management reports. This large chunk of the day represents time not used performing the job they were hired to do. One organization hired engineers and economists to do fieldwork. Yet because of all the reports and revised reports that had to be filed after each field visit, these researchers spent only one-third of their time in the field and the other two-thirds filling out field reports.

Part of the role of the leader is to deflect as much of this administrative nonwork as possible. Leaders can create management systems that filter out the unnecessary and seemingly innocuous requests and demands that snowball into endless hours of work.

214

In one electronics company, the manager of R&D developed an extremely effective method of handling administrative requests. A simple request for information by the CEO often snowballed into hours of work for those on the lower rungs of the corporate ladder, especially if it required collecting or analyzing data outside the normal requirements. Every time this manager received such a request, she would calculate the cost in dollars, hours, and schedule setbacks on key R&D projects. Before she acted on the requests, she would send these calculations back up the chain, asking if she was still to proceed in light of the costs. The number of requests dropped drastically as she protected her staff from interruptions in their work.

At times, leaders may simply need to leave their followers alone. One of the greatest impediments to productivity is constant interruption. Several exemplary followers told me how they moved their offices to protect themselves from their bosses. When they were next door or across the hall, the boss would barge in or call over to them without any thought of the followers' work progress. They became on-call sounding boards for ideas or dumping grounds for delegation. Once they moved further away, they had longer periods to concentrate on their work.

Besides removing productivity roadblocks, leaders can encourage self-management in followers. For example, in an electronics firm, the followers design, schedule, and monitor the work in each semi-autonomous work group. They hold weekly meetings with the department leader for briefings on progress and problems. They identify critical issues for the leader and suggest the steps to resolve them, especially if the issues involve other departments. This self-management allows the leader to attend to activities that are important at the division or company level or are best handled at the leader's administrative level.

These self-managed followers require fewer bosses, yielding a considerable payroll savings, and they often set higher productivity goals than management does. At one plant, the workers schedule, operate, and maintain the plant so well that no managers are even present during the night shift.

Another example of self-management relates to problem solving. People closest to the problem are given responsibility to solve it. They make the decision and have to live with it. Dean Ruwe, president of Copeland Corporation, a maker of refrigeration and air-conditioning products, discovered that "if you have 1,000 problem identifiers [followers] but only supervisors [leaders] can solve problems, you've got an overload in the system." Consequently, Copeland tells its workers to gather their own data so they can solve the problems themselves.

For example, a drill bit operator at Copeland collected data about two drill bits. The one the company wanted him to use cost $4.50. An alternative cost $9.00. He showed that the $9.00 bit produced three times as much at only twice the cost. Unlike the cheaper bit, it didn't break off in the product's deep holes, thus reducing damaged goods and downtime. He single-handedly sold the company on the more expensive bit. Not only did he receive company-wide recognition, but the story of his problem solving is now part of the company's folklore.

Just as exemplary followers want to manage themselves, they have no desire to actively monitor the leader's work progress. As partners, they want a relationship of equals who trust each other. Despite all the hubbub surrounding participative management, exemplary followers don't want to know the trivia of the leader's job. Nor do they want involvement in every decision. Instead, followers want involvement only in decisions which may affect them in direct and important ways.

While followers self-manage their individual work, leaders can help manage the "cracks" that fall between the technical work of different followers. As followers immerse themselves in their technical area, important interdependencies may get overlooked. By monitoring and integrating the work flow, the leader can make sure that the organization's efforts come together.

One manager I know posts a "picturegraph" in the coffee room illustrating the sequence and flow of work assignments. As individuals or teams complete their discrete tasks, they fill in the part of the picture that represents their contribution. As people get coffee, they can instantly learn the status of the department's work, which employees are on schedule, who might need some extra help, and what bottlenecks might occur.

Leaders can also serve as "synergy catalysts" who create and broker networks. Many major scientific breakthroughs are the result of some form of synergy or cross-fertilization from other fields. Individuals can experience individual breakthroughs as well as personal development by coming into contact with other creative, hardworking peers.

Leaders are in a position to see the big picture—all the various talents and projects that the subordinates are actively pursuing. If two followers are separated by organizational structure, time zones, cultural background, or fields of expertise, they may never know that their individual work has a bearing on the other's. Leaders can provide the network by means of which these talented people can put their heads together and come up with significant products or progress.

For example, the vice president of an aerospace company was very supportive of a personnel manager's development of innovative human-resource programs. He put the manager in touch with a manager in the engineering department who, as a result of her natural manner with people, had a high-productivity, high-morale work force. The vice president thought the pair would spark each other's creativity, resulting in higher-quality people programs for the entire company. His expectations were met as the engineering department became the testing ground for many programs that, after their initial success, spread throughout the company.

Similarly, leaders can facilitate followers forming into a team. Many managers believe if you put people in the same room, a highly functioning team will result. Yet most football teams practice forty hours a week, executing plays together, identifying group mistakes, and talking over plans and strategies to prepare for a three-hour game on Sunday.

Few work groups engage in similar activities, even though they have to perform together forty hours per week instead of just three on Sunday. They do not review past actions. They rarely join together to learn from their mistakes, practice together, set new goals, or build up their team spirit. Any training workers do receive is individual in nature; one worker attends a seminar on a specific subject. This would be equivalent to a football team sending its quarterbacks to New York, its centers to Chicago, and its ends to Los Angeles to receive individualized instruction in their separate specialties. How could we expect them to perform as a team come opening game?

The leader can add value by using their interpersonal skills to get a team off the ground. Compare the team-building styles of two successive leaders. The government relations office of a major oil company was filled with dissatisfaction and dissension. The head of the office ran it in old-fashioned dictatorial style. She assigned the professional staff to relatively menial tasks while saving all meaningful lobbying work for herself. She seldom consulted the staff on strategy, yet she often unilaterally changed their work assignments and schedules. If she made a mistake, she found a convenient scapegoat to blame it on. In addition, having come up by the public affairs route, she treated the legal staff in the office as second-class citizens. Since the legal staff reported to the general counsel back at headquarters and not to her, most staff members felt she went out of her way to provoke them. For instance, when one of her staff had a conflict with an attorney, rather than help the two people resolve it, she sided with her subordinate. Needless to say, her emotional bank account was overdrawn. Unfortunately for her, the office flubbed a major piece of legislation, and she was replaced.

The new boss took an entirely different approach. He got the entire staff—both public affairs and legal—involved in planning the office's strategy. He broke them into mixed teams, each of which would handle all aspects of one major piece of legislation, including lobbying. Each Monday and Friday they had staff meetings to brief each other on progress and contacts made. When conflicts arose within a team or between teams, he made it clear that it was their responsibility to work things out. If they needed his assistance, they must first present him with their proposal for resolving the conflict. He gave credit for success where it was due and made sure the entire office shared the limelight.

In summary, leaders do not create environments where exemplary followers flourish by simply decreeing that it will happen. This results in followership being no more than a pleasant conceit to which leaders can pay lip service but no dues. Instead, the best leaders build followership into the fabric of the organizational structure and culture by:

- Orientation programs that stress the importance of exemplary followership;
- Training programs that teach and hone the skills of exemplary followers;
- Performance evaluation systems that rate how the individual carries out the followership role;
- Reward systems that underscore the importance of exemplary followership;
- Rotational programs whereby people move back and forth between followership and leadership roles;
- Role modeling wherein the leader assumes the followership role and demonstrates exemplary followership skills; and
- Leadership activities that specifically encourage exemplary followership, such as team-building, removing roadblocks to a follower's productivity, or being a synergy catalyst.

Be Less a Hero and More a Hero Maker

A reporter once asked Ray Kroc of McDonald's fame what the measure of success is. After pausing to think, he answered that many people measure success by how many millions of dollars they made. His own personal measure, though, was the number of millionaires he helped make.

Some leaders need to be heroes. Others are hero makers. In their book *SuperLeadership,* Charles Manz and Henry Sims discuss how the former focus the attention on themselves at the expense of the followers. All power and vision are vested in them, while followers are merely empty vessels. They try to foster dependence on them by capitalizing on an artificial sense of their own superiority.

Hero makers, on the other hand, understand that the strong pillars that support the organization for the long haul are the exemplary followers. Power, vision, and success necessarily rest with these followers, who ensure that the system continues even when the leader is gone.

Exemplary followers clearly prefer hero makers to heroes. This does not imply that they want to be the hero at the leader's expense. Instead, it is the leader's attitude and emphasis that they evaluate. Is the leader primarily interested in her or his success? Do they arrange things so that they get all the choice work and public recognition? Or do they take a partnership approach where we work together to make sure that we all succeed along with the organization?

Being a hero maker means enabling followers to

actually *be* the "strong pillars" that support the organization and that receive admiration for their work. Leaders initially do this by giving followers important critical path work that engages and challenges their talents. In fact, most, if not all, of the critical path work should be turned over to followers. This not only focuses their efforts at the heart of the enterprise but also enables the organization to carry on in the leader's absence.

In determining how to conduct critical path work, the leader should listen to the followers. Not only are they usually closer to the day-to-day issues involved in implementation; they must be committed to the eventual path. Fred Rogers of *Mister Rogers' Neighborhood* remembers his father's advice: "When your workers have a plan that will work as well as your plan to reach the goal, use theirs, since they are the ones who will devote the energy to making it work. If your force yours on them, the workers will rightfully resent it."

Likewise, leaders should be sensitive to the personal dreams that followers bring to the organization. Besides working toward the organizational goal, followers might want exposure to certain activities, to learn new skills or get involved in professional associations. Just as leaders want followers to help them achieve their goals, leaders need to return the favor.

Leaders can start by asking followers what their personal goals are and what they can do to help. As opportunities arise, mesh those personal goals with organizational needs. Use your contacts on behalf of the follower. To the extent that you help further their personal dreams, you are a hero maker.

Remember to give public recognition to followers for their contributions and achievements. I remember a large national meeting where Senator Daniel Inouye of

Hawaii was invited to answer questions about a report his office had written on mental health policy. The report had received much public praise and support as a national model. When it came time for the question-and-answer session with the senator, he told the audience that he appreciated their support. However, he had not researched or written the report—his legislative aide had done this. He then introduced his aide to the meeting and turned the Q&A session over to him. For the next thirty minutes, the aide held center stage, both demonstrating his competence and receiving full credit for his contribution.

Hero makers like Senator Inouye know when to lead and when to follow. Few bosses are good at this transition. In describing his boss, one exemplary follower said, "Her leadership switch is always on. She's forgotten where her followership switch is." Leaders need to be fluid, coming to the foreground when needed and receding to the background when not needed. A follower's technical expertise will make him or her the appropriate person to lead for a time. At that point, the leader should yield and become a follower.

In *Leadership Is an Art,* Max DePree describes how difficult it is for established leaders to allow subordinates to break custom and assume the leadership role. He calls these subordinates "roving leaders" because they play the follower role most of the time but emerge as leaders when needed. According to DePree, "roving leaders are those indispensable people who are there when we need them . . . the hierarchical leader is obliged to identify the roving leader, then to support and follow him or her, and also to exhibit the grace that enables the roving leader to lead."

To know when to lead and when to follow, leaders

need to understand when each role is appropriate. Sociologist A. W. Gouldner proposed a useful distinction between "locals" and "cosmopolitans." Locals primarily serve and are loyal to the organization and its goals, norms, and values. Cosmopolitans identify more with their profession and its values, work standards, and criteria for success.

As a general rule, exemplary followers look to leaders to exert more "local" leadership while the followers represent more the "cosmopolitan" side. The leaders' expertise lies more with understanding the needs and constraints of the organization, while the followers' contribution is professional expertise. The leader is like the organizational glue that solidifies the multiple contributions of followers.

Leaders, then, should lead when the issues pertain to the organization. They are at the helm for goal setting, work distribution, resource gathering, organizational interfaces, and other organizational necessities. They serve as a reality check for followers on whether or not ideas will fly within the organization. They let followers know what the organizational needs and limits are.

For their part, followers take the lead on matters related to technical or professional expertise. When a vital computer breaks down in a bank, it is the computer specialist, not the boss, who takes charge in getting it running again. When deciding what testing equipment to buy for quality control, the technician who will use it takes the lead.

Hierarchical and roving leaders might hand off to each other several times during the same meeting when both technical and organizational matters are at stake. By sticking to their relative areas of expertise, the transition from one to the other is much more smooth.

So leaders are hero makers when they enable followers to take the lead at appropriate times. This switching is comparable to what happens in a jazz band. The feature performer—a trumpeter, let's say— may have more time in the spotlight, while the others accompany her softly in the background. But when another performer gets a solo, it doesn't take away from the lead. Instead, it enhances the entire performance for the group, as well as the audience. A good jazz group knows that both the band members and the audience get bored if all they heard was the trumpet all night. It also would look ridiculous if the trumpeter took the piano player's spot to do solos on the piano. Instead, a smooth jazz group passes the lead among its members so deftly that the audience may not even notice. They are so attuned to each other's music that they can follow one lead, switch to another, and then take the lead —all while keeping track of the overall flow of the music toward its conclusion.

On a different level, University of California, Berkeley, researchers Todd LaPorte, Gene Rochlin, and Karlene Roberts have studied complex organizations, like aircraft carriers and electric utilities. These organizations' activities have almost no margin for error. When things don't go right, lives can be lost. The researchers wanted to know how these organizations achieve remarkably low failure rates. Their findings are turning traditional management thinking on its ear. For instance, the belief that in crises or periods of peak emergency a strong leader with strict chain-of-command systems works best is dead wrong.

These high-reliability organizations have their leaders and technical specialists, just like any other organization. But the same individual may play different roles under different circumstances.

As in most organizations, during stress-free times the leaders are in charge and the technical specialists play follower. Most followers are focused day to day on their work and have little desire to lead. They expect the leader to keep the organization running smoothly. But when stress hits—an F-14 Tomcat is landing at midnight on a nuclear aircraft carrier or lightning knocks out a major transformer, causing a burnout—roles change. According to one report:

> The most striking and surprising role change occurs in the white heat of danger, when the entire system threatens to collapse. Then cogs can become big wheels. Whatever their status in the formal hierarchy, they are trained intensively every day so that—based on their expertise—they can take complete command, redirect operations or bring them to an abrupt halt. The system works. It comes under greatest strain when top executives remote from front-line action issue unrealistic orders to people down the line.

During a mission, an aircraft carrier will launch twenty-one planes at fifty-second intervals. A plane is rolled into position, checked from top to bottom, and catapulted just in time for another plane to land. Such precision demands almost perfect teamwork. Such teamwork requires that everyone do his or her job, while trusting all others to do theirs—partnership in action.

One might expect that such complex organizations would require very experienced leaders and teams who have worked together over long periods. The reality is that the top twenty officers and most of the 5,000 enlisted personnel are on board for less than three years. It is the 300 petty officers, the middle and lower management, who have the long aircraft carrier experience. According to the researchers: "Their collective experience is the ship's memory; they run the show."

The Future of Leading

Leadership as defined by exemplary followers differs considerably from the myth espoused by leadership enthusiasts. Leaders are partners who simply do different things than followers. But both add value and both contributions are necessary for success. But one is not more important than the other.

Frequently, I encounter top technical people who desperately want to get promoted to a management job. They are lured into leadership positions by the power over decisions and people, visibility, higher pay, and inclusion in the inner circle. Many of these people are great followers and technical contributors.

I try to point out to them that most people who get promoted to the management ladder only advance one or two rungs. Rather than be stuck in a technical job they like, they are going to be stuck in a low-level management job they may dislike, earning slightly more money. Instead of spending twenty-five years in a technical job, they will spend twenty years as a first-level supervisor, with almost no real power. Is this really what they want?

What these followers don't realize is that they may not be suited to the actual work required of leaders. Their focus will become organizational issues, rather than technical.

In two informal surveys, I asked subordinates to rate their leaders on two questions: were they good at leading and did they like the job? In both surveys, only 25 percent of the leaders met both conditions.

In a companion survey, I asked the leaders how many would go back to their nonleader jobs if they could without a loss of face. Seventy-five percent said they would. One manager summarized her experience: "I traded in exciting professional work to spend 90 percent of my time deciding whether my people should have twelve- or fourteen-foot offices, what the vacation schedule should be, and who should get the 2 percent merit increase that isn't enough to motivate anyone anyway. I spend so much time on administrivia crises that I don't have time for people or managing."

While I do not know if the 75 percent who are unsuitable leaders are identical to the 75 percent who are dissatisfied, the statistics alone ensure that at least 50 percent of them are the same. Thus, many in leadership positions—at least one of every two in my informal surveys and perhaps as high as three out of four—should not be there and do not want to be there. The odds of their success are not very high, especially if they are mainly doing it for the extrinsic rewards, rather than the work itself.

Although there is no shortage of people who want to lead, there is a real shortage of people who can and want to do the actual work of leaders. I have watched even skilled managers return to their technical work because they found it less stressful and more gratifying.

Although the personal costs of leadership positions are glossed over by the leadership books and the executive recruiters, they are real nonetheless. As one executive put it, "I missed my kids' birthdays, ball games, and parent-teacher meetings. I was seldom there for the joy or the tears. When it came time to give away my children at their weddings, I realized I knew my business and my subordinates better than I knew my own kids."

More organizations are becoming like university departments, where faculty members have to be cajoled to be department heads. These faculty see very little personal gain from the experience and a huge drain on their time. In some universities, the faculty members rotate the position among themselves so that no one has to serve for too long. Each takes a turn in the spirit of organizational citizenship rather than professional interest.

The Payoff for Exemplary Leaders

The goal of exemplary leadership is not merely to attract followers. Many leaders, whether dictators or democrats, whether charismatic or matter-of-fact, can build a following. The ultimate test of leadership is the quality of the followers. Exemplary leaders attract exemplary followers. As co-adventurers, they embark on a worthwhile journey together. They rely on each other to arrive there safely and successfully.

One American executive related a conversation with a high-ranking Japanese counterpart. The Japanese told him, "If I point my hand to the north and say 'Go,' four thousand employees will obediently march, even over a cliff." The American responded, "If I were to point my arm north and say 'Go,' four thousand hands would move my arm to the northeast or northwest so that we avoid going over the cliff."

Ordinary leaders go over cliffs—sometimes from their own arrogance, other times from being pushed by resentful followers. Exemplary leaders seldom get close to cliffs, not with exemplary followers to point them in the right direction.

Postscript:

The Future of Following

Followership and leadership can be thought of as a partnership that simultaneously reaches back and reaches forward in time. We know something about our heritage, although it is skewed with its emphasis on leadership. But what about tomorrow—what is the future of followership?

The Right and Responsibility
to Choose a Worthy Leader

It is up to us to decide whom we will follow. Jared Diamond, an anthropologist at UCLA, learned this lesson from a nearly fatal boat accident which occurred shortly after his arrival by plane in New Guinea:

> At the dock outside the plane terminal I saw a row of long dugout canoes with big outboard motors, flimsy awnings, and pushy young men each trying to hustle newly arrived passengers into his canoe. I selected a canoe whose cocky driver proceeded to roar out into the strait at full throttle through high waves.
>
> Several miles from shore, water began to crash into the canoe, which suddenly capsized, nearly trapping us inside. Two crew members swam off with the sole life preservers, leaving me and the other five passengers trying to cling to the upturned bottom of the canoe's smooth round hull as it pitched in the waves. Luckily, just before sunset, we were spotted and picked up by two small sailcanoes out fishing. One of them then capsized under the weight of its added passengers, who were never found; the other, with me and the remaining passengers, reached Sorong. There I learned that several similar accidents had occurred recently.
>
> My initial reaction was to blame the idiotic driver whose recklessness had almost cost me my life, and the Sorong harbor police who licensed

such idiots. Of course it was all their fault! Then I happened to run into Bill Brown, a Cornell biologist who had also just arrived. When I told him of my close escape, he replied that he had taken one look at those canoes and pushy young drivers, decided they were dangerous, and waited for a slow, safe tugboat.

I realized that I hadn't been a powerless victim of that idiotic boatman. There was something simple I could have done to avoid the accident: not get into that canoe. More generally, I understood that I had ultimate responsibility for my safety.

As followers, we have the right to decide who we will follow. But finding a worthy leader is no easy task. It requires analysis, judgment, and some risk-taking. If no leader meets our criteria, we have the right not to follow. But once we decide, then we also must accept the corresponding responsibility for that decision.

This right and responsibility has many facets. On occasion, we may need to encourage worthy leaders to play their roles. For instance, before moving into Hull House, Jane Addams got cold feet about her plan to open a settlement house in the slums of Chicago. She wanted to remain in the physical and emotional comfort of her family. It was Ellen Starr, her first follower, who pushed and prodded Addams to take the lead in realizing their dream. Had it not been for Starr's support at this crucial moment, Addams might never have made the break with her past. Instead she would have played the "maiden aunt" role that was the common fate of college-educated women in the late 1800s.

As followers, we also should be actively involved in

the selection process. "Democracy," George Bernard Shaw observed, "ensures we shall be governed no better than we deserve." When only 34 percent of the population exercise their right to vote in presidential elections, the 66 percent of nonvoters relinquish their right to complain about the leader. If we want high quality leaders, we must seize control of the selection process.

A final facet of our followership rights and responsibilities is to know when to stop supporting a leader. Regardless of how hard we try to find worthy leaders, we will make occasional mistakes. After we work with the leader to try to improve his or her performance, we may conclude it is a lost cause. Rather than continue to support an undeserving leader, we have the right and responsibility to cut our losses by removing our support. Although leaders have power over followers, it continues only as long as the followers allow. Since it is the followers who keep leaders in power, they can take away that power. As Chester Barnard wrote in *Functions of the Executive,* "the decision as to whether an order has authority or not lies with the person to whom it is addressed, and does not reside in 'persons of authority' or those who issue orders."

The Right and Responsibility
to Act Without Leaders

Not far from my house in Pittsburgh stands the Highland Park Super Playground—a living monument to followership. A group of neighbors decided that this huge city park could use a modern playground that captured the imagination of kids. Their dream was a structure

234

where children of all ages and from all over the city could explore, play, and learn.

When they first took their dream to the city leaders, they were turned away. They then planned the structure on their own, and raised $100,000 to build it. On a spring weekend, they invited Pittsburgh residents to bring their tools and selves to construct the playground. In barn-raising fashion, hundreds of citizens built the structure in three days. The citizens also monitor and maintain it. Thousands of children use the Super Playground, while its unique design has turned it into a local tourist attraction.

Vaclav Havel, the poet-dissident who became Czechoslovakia's first elected president after the overthrow of the communist regime, captured this phenomenon of action without leaders in *The Power of the Powerless*. His thesis is that followers hold significant power, even in totalitarian states, but only if they act on it. Havel gives the example of how ordinary citizens, like local greengrocers, have a responsibility to act in the absence of valid leadership. At a minimum, they can refuse to show signs of support of the dictatorship, for example by not putting flags in the window. Their actions might escalate into collective efforts to protect themselves. These, then, might blossom into open opposition and the seizing of their legitimate right to self-government.

Havel's greengrocers and the Super Playground builders remind us that each of us can aspire to exemplary followership, regardless of how our traditional leaders perform. We need not wait for leaders to lead, nor for society to bless followership. Too many societal institutions have a vested interest in keeping the spot-

235

light on leadeship—on the form rather than the substance of success. They would rather focus on a Churchill, even though when asked about Britain's success in World War II, Churchill himself replied, "The nation was the lion and had the lion's heart. I only had the luck to give the roar."

The power of followership is ours—a social birthright—but only if we assume the responsibilities that accompany it. A nation of exemplary followers makes a government of wolves impossible.

Exemplary followers are like the leaf in the Magritte painting on the cover of this book. His leaf is not only a part of the tree but embodies the entire tree. His tree-within-the-leaf depicts the essence of exemplary followers. They embody the spirit, the purpose, and the direction of the whole organization. Imagine the potential of an organization blessed with these fully engaged, fully energized, fully thinking followers. Organizations populated with these exemplary followers who exercise their rights and who more than fulfill their responsibilities are not only possible, but necessary for success in the next century.

The rights and responsibilities of exemplary followership will shape much of followership's future. But much is still unknown and awaits discovery. I am reminded of the maps used by Lewis and Clark as they searched for an inland water route across the United States to the Pacific Ocean. As they conquered the territory, they drew new maps to reflect the new geography. Each new map had much more detail about the "known" land than the unknown frontier. But each map also depicted the frontier optimistically, yet naively; it was drawn as a small strip of land with few geographical obstacles. In reality, of course, the unknown frontier was much rougher and larger—a bigger and bolder challenge than they could envision.

So it is with our journey into followership. Through this book, I tried to push back the frontier of followership to make it more approachable, more personal, more inspiring. I tried to capture the major landmarks so that you can journey with me into the topic. But, like Lewis and Clark's frontier, we have only begun to explore the vast, powerful world of followership.

Acknowledgments

I am thankful to the many people who have helped make this book possible.

Pat Chew, a professor at the University of Pittsburgh Law School, has collaborated with me over the last eighteen years. This book dominated much of our lives during the last five years. Without her, it would be nothing more than a nifty idea inside my head. When the initial book proposal was turned down, she encouraged and helped me redraft it for resubmission. When my spirits sagged, she buoyed them. When my thinking got fuzzy, she restored logic. When I needed time, she made it happen. Her insights helped guide the research and conclusions, while her personal example of exemplary followership provided a constant role model. She read and critiqued every word on every page. Most of all, she kept reminding me that the book was important and that I should not stop until I could be proud of it.

Harriet Rubin, my editor at Currency Books of Doubleday, is a champion in bringing much-needed fresh ideas to the business world. She believed enough in me and this book to include it on her list. She cared enough about the book's usefulness and success that she made me rewrite and rewrite until it met her standards. I have never met a better advocate for the reader. Janet Coleman and Lynn Fenwick were also helpful on a day-to-day basis, alternating between the follower and leader roles quite capably. Nancy Evans supported the book in its initial stages during her tenure as president of Doubleday.

Syed Shariq lent his considerable intellectual prowess to the book's premise and to several chapters. Paul Brophy, Janet Nordin, Howard Seckler, Stu Mechlin, Ellen Mechlin, and Art Caplan read early articles or drafts and gave me the benefit of their thinking. Conversations with Gene Schmitz, Don Green, D. J. O'Laughlin, and Bill Andrews honed my thinking considerably. Dick Raymond and Bob Doyle continue to be valuable sounding boards. Rev. Demetrius Dumm of St. Vincent's College provided valuable insight into the nature of discipleship. Dr. Shirley Williams of the College of St. Francis introduced me to the concept of "enoughness." Professor Jules Lobel of the University of Pittsburgh School of Law provided me with the Bertolt Brecht poem.

Janet Nordin of AT&T was one of the first people to recognize the "power of followership" and asked me to discuss it with her managers and supervisors. Janet Nordin, Don Leonard, Howard Seckler, Dave Carney, Tom Cruz, Dan Carroll, Judy Lindner, Carol Bidrawn, Dick Carline, John Janik, and Jerry W. Johnson of Bell Laboratories provided a setting to test out the ideas over a five-year period.

Janet Caplan and Dick Hayes teamed up with me on the Bell Labs project, which resulted in the "Productivity Enhancement Groups" (PEG). Janet Caplan collaborated on shaping and refining all the PEG concepts, including the followership material which made the PEG program such a success. She also supported significantly my effort to complete this book. Ron DeLange, Bonnie Prokopowicz, Joe Halter, Doug Newlin, Eric Kampmeier, Steve Sentoff, Steve Miranda, the PEG cotrainers, and the PEG participants—all of Bell Labs— critiqued the application of the ideas.

Tim McGuire, Betsy Bailey, Ilker Baybars, and Bob Sullivan provide me with the opportunity to teach at the Graduate School of Industrial Administration of Carnegie-Mellon University. They particularly support my innovating new courses that mesh creative approaches with real-world business needs. I also appreciate the interaction and support of my colleagues on the faculty of GSIA.

Teresa Sokol from the Public Relations Department

at Carnegie-Mellon has ably generated media interest in followership. Similarly, Alan Webber and Tom Teal of the *Harvard Business Review* deserve credit for publishing my seminal article "In Praise of Followers," which became one of *HBR*'s top twenty-five best-selling reprints. In addition, the *Wall Street Journal,* the *Los Angeles Times,* the *Chicago Tribune,* the *Atlanta Constitution, Nation's Business, Board Room Reports, Training Magazine, Working Women, PC Week, Health Care Forum,* and *Executive Report* have published stories about my work.

Carol Mann, my book agent, has represented me for three books, being a valuable contact point in the world of publishing.

The Leigh Bureau, my lecture agency, has provided numerous opportunities for me to talk about followership. Bill Leigh, Danny Stern, Les Tuerk, Ron Szymanski, Larry Leson, Tom Neilssen, and Fern Weber have consistently supported my work.

Joan Krueger, Gene Mainelli, Ray Hock, Mark Bickhard, Jack Hautaluoma, and Chuck Neidt are teachers who believed in me and whose lessons continue to guide me. They gave me a personal experience with the positive effects of mentoring.

Bonnie Schultz, Gail Knowlan, Karen DeCamp, and Nancy Reed provided encouragement, good humor, and fast, high-quality word-processing during the multiple drafts and long days of working under the book deadline. They shifted their schedules, worked overtime and weekends, put up with my stress, and critiqued what they typed—all to help me turn out the best book possible. Amelia Giles, Eleanor Balouk, Barb Carlson, and Karen Poole provided backup support at critical times.

Acknowledgments

Erica Levy, Sigmunde Sommers Freed, Dave Levy, Christopher Tang, and Lisa Leonardo contributed considerable value as research assistants during the course of this book.

My family continues to be the most important wellspring of inspiration and support. Pat, Luke, and Lauren provide a reason, a home, smiles, hugs, and many joys. While most of my personal followership and leadership styles were forged with my parents, brothers, and sisters-in-law, my much larger and extended family continues to teach me valuable lessons. Family members confirmed the book's title when I wavered.

Thank you to all of you.

Notes

Warning: Leadership May Be Hazardous for You

PAGE

7–8   *"Leaders contribute on the average . . ."*

G. R. Salancik and J. Pfeffer, "Constraints on Administrative Discretion: The Limited Influence of Mayors on City Budgets," *Urban Affairs Quarterly,* 12 (1977), pp. 474–98.

J. Pfeffer, "The Ambiguity of Leadership," *Academy of Management Review,* 2 (1977), 104–12.

James R. Meindl, Sanford B. Ehrlich, and Janet M. Dukerich, "The Romance of Leadership," *Administrative Science Quarterly,* 30 (1985), pp. 78–102.

Walter Kiechel III, "The Case Against Leaders," *Fortune,* November 21, 1988, pp. 217–20.

Gary A. Yukl, *Leadership in Organizations* (Englewood Cliffs, N.J.: Prentice Hall, 1981, 1989).

Michael McGill, *American Business and the Quick Fix* (New York: Henry Holt, 1988).

F. G. Bailey, *Humbuggery and Manipulation* (Ithaca, N.Y.: Cornell University Press, 1988).

Not all writers agree with this view. For an alternative interpretation, read

Gary A. Yukl, *Leadership in Organizations* (2nd ed.) (Englewood Cliffs, N.J.: Prentice Hall, 1981, 1989).

D. V. Day and G. R. Lord, "Executive Leadership and Organizational Performance," *Journal of Management,* 14 (September 1990), p. 453.

N. Weiner and T. A. Mahoney, "A Model of Corporate Performance as a Function of Environmental, Organizational, and Leadership Influence," *Academy of Management Journal,* 24, 1981, pp. 453–470.

9   *"Witt Stephens, an investment banker . . ."*

James Morgan, "Wily Varmints," *Investment Vision* (June/July 1991), pp. 64–69.

Notes

1. If the People Will Lead, the Leaders Will Follow

PAGE

14 ". . . *former Stanford University president* . . ."
Donald Kennedy, "Learning, Thinking, Believing," *Stanford Magazine*, September 1990, pp. 27–29.

15 *"Warren Bennis, a respected leadership guru* . . ."
Warren Bennis, *On Becoming a Leader* (Reading, Mass.: Addison-Wesley, 1989).

17 ". . . *10,000 published leadership studies* . . ."
Gary A. Yukl, *Leadership in Organizations* (Englewood Cliffs, N.J.: Prentice Hall, 1981, 1989).

20 *"The leader's effect on organizational success* . . ."
G. R. Salancik and J. Pfeffer, "Constraints on Administrative Discretion: The Limited Influence of Mayors on City Budgets," *Urban Affairs Quarterly*, 12 (1977), pp. 474–98.
J. Pfeffer, "The Ambiguity of Leadership," *Academy of Management Review*, 2 (1977), 104–12.
James R. Meindl, Sanford B. Ehrlich, and Janet M. Dukerich, "The Romance of Leadership," *Administrative Science Quarterly*, 30 (1985), pp. 78–102.
Yukl, op. cit.
Walter Kiechel III, "The Case Against Leaders," *Fortune*, November 21, 1988, pp. 217–20.
Michael E. McGill, *American Business and the Quick Fix* (New York: Henry Holt, 1988).
F. G. Bailey, *Humbuggery and Manipulation* (Ithaca, N.Y.: Cornell University Press, 1988).

20 *"As Walter Kiechel of Fortune* . . ."
Kiechel, op. cit.

24 *"John Adams confirms this* . . ."
Lawrence G. Gipson, *The Coming of the Revolution* (New York: Harper & Row, 1954).

31–32 *"Who built the seven gates* . . ."
Bertolt Brecht: Selected Poems (New York: Harcourt, Brace, 1947), p. 109.

2. The Difference Between Success and Failure in the 21st Century Organization

PAGE

35 *"Survival of the fittest pits* . . ." Richard Hofstadter, *Social Darwinism in American Thought,* revised edition (New York: G. Braziller, 1969).

48 *"Nobody outside of the Continental Congress* . . ."
Fawn M. Brodie, *Thomas Jefferson: An Intimate History* (New York: Norton, 1974).

Notes

53   *"Many women residents of Jane Addam's Hull-House . . ."*
Allen F. Davis, *American Heroine: The Life and Legend of Jane Addams* (New York: Oxford University Press, 1973).

3. Why Become a Follower?

54   *"Since developing leadership is . . ."*
William Litzinger and Thomas Schaefer, "Leadership Through Followership," *Business Horizons,* September–October 1982, pp. 78–81.

55   *"China's 'mandarin court' system . . ."*
Edward C. Page, *Political Authority and Bureaucratic Power: A Comparative Analysis* (Knoxville: University of Tennessee Press, 1985).

E. A. Kracke, Jr., "Family vs. Merit in Chinese Civil Service Examinations under the Empire," in *Studies of Governmental Institutions in Chinese History,* edited by John L. Bishop (Cambridge, Mass.: Harvard University Press, 1968), pp. 171–94.

Wang Yu-Chuan, "An Outline of the Central Government of the Former Han Dynasty," in ibid., pp. 1–56.

Harry Harding, *Organizing China: The Problem of Bureaucracy 1949–1976* (Stanford, Calif.: Stanford University Press, 1981).

57   *". . . having read Plato's dialogues . . ."*
Aristotle, *The Politics,* edited by Steven Everson (Cambridge University Press, 1988).

57   *"According to Jonathan Barnes . . ."*
Jonathan Barnes, *Aristotle* (Oxford University Press, 1982).

62   *"Abraham Zaleznik . . ."*
Abraham Zaleznik, "Managers and Leaders: Are They Different?" *Harvard Business Review,* May–June 1977, pp. 67–78.

68   *"For example, Jane Addams, Julia Lathrop . . ."*
Allen F. Davis, op. cit.

70   *"When Pat Riley was the coach of . . ."*
Dean Ornish, *Dr. Dean Ornish's Program for Reversing Heart Disease* (New York: Random House, 1990), p. 222.

71   *"Leonard Peikoff, the protector of Ayn Rand's . . ."*
Nathaniel Branden, *Judgment Day: My Years with Ayn Rand* (Boston: Houghton Mifflin, 1989).

71   *"At the center of the code of Bushido . . ."*
Daidoji Yuzan, *The Code of the Samurai,* translated by A. L. Sadler (Rutland, Vt.: Charles E. Tuttle, 1941, 1988).

Inazo Nitobe, *Bushido: The Soul of Japan* (Rutland, Vt.: Charles E. Tuttle, 1969).

Notes

72   *"Consider Sancho Panza, the squire . . ."*
      Dale Wasserman, *Man of La Mancha* (New York: Random House, 1966).
75   *". . . William Broyles describes how the Vietcong . . ."*
      William Broyles, Jr., *Brothers in Arms: A Journey from War to Peace* (New York: Alfred A. Knopf, 1986).

4. Enoughness

PAGE
80   *"Rachel Carson, the author of . . ."*
      Lewis Amster, "Rachel Louise Carson," *American Reformers,* edited by Alden Whitman (New York: H. W. Wilson, 1985).
80   *"The Jewel Tea Company . . ."*
      Abraham Zaleznik, "Managers and Leaders: Are They Different?" *Harvard Business Review,* May–June 1977, pp. 67–78.
83   *". . . 'enoughness.' This term comes from the Samoans."*
      Professor Shirley Williams of the College of St. Francis in Joliet, Illinois gleaned the concept of "enoughness" from her research on public education in Hawaii. She introduced me to it and its relationship to followership.

5. Identifying Your Followership Style

PAGE
93   *". . . Adler had an 'anti-doctrinaire nature . . .' "*
      Irving Stone, *Passions of the Mind* (New York: Doubleday, 1971).
94   *"A recent article in* Government Executive *. . ."*
      G. Ronald Gilbert, "Effective Leaders Must Be Good Followers Too," *Government Executive,* June 1990, p. 58.
100   *"Barry Paris, the biographer of Greta Garbo . . ."*
      Jeff Sewald, "A Writer's Life," *Pittsburgh Magazine,* July 1991, pp. 24–46.
103   *"In one survey, I found . . ."*
      Robert E. Kelley, *The Gold-Collar Worker* (Reading, Mass.: Addison-Wesley, 1985).
      Robert E. Kelley, "Gold-Collar Worker Survey," unpublished summary, Carnegie-Mellon University, 1990.
      Labor Letter, "Trust and Loyalty Run Low at American Companies," *Wall Street Journal,* January 16, 1990, p. A1.
      Carol Hymowitz, "Many Middle Managers Find Bosses Uninspiring," *Wall Street Journal,* November 6, 1989, p. B1.
105   *"As Daniel Goleman reported . . ."*
      Daniel Goleman, "Agreeable or Anger," *New York Times Magazine,* April 16, 1989, p. 20.

Notes

James Morgan, "Fifty Ways to Lose Your Languor," *American Way,* August 1991, pp. 57–83.

109   *"Red Auerbach, formerly coach . . ."*
Arnold "Red" Auerbach, "Misleading Followers," *Harvard Business Review,* January–February 1989, p. 152.

112   *"Conformists lack what St. Theresa . . ."*
This story was told to me by Rev. Demetrius Dumm, an expert on discipleship, of St. Vincent's College in Latrobe, Pa.

118   *"In 1989, when Kodak . . ."*
Claire Ansberry and Peter Pae, "Kodak's Cost-Cutting Bid Brings Yawn on Wall Street but Concern in Hometown," *Wall Street Journal,* August 25, 1989, p. A4.

120   *"Dante wrote in the Inferno . . ."*
Dante, *Inferno,* translated by Mark Musa (Bloomington: Indiana University Press, 1971), p. 21.

121   *"According to Dick McDonald . . ."*
Ellen Graham, "McDonald's Pickle: He Began Fast Food but Gets No Credit," *Wall Street Journal,* August 15, 1991, p. A1.

123   "Red Auerbach of the Boston Celtics . . ."
Auerbach, loc. cit.

6. The Skills of Exemplary Followers

PAGE

128   *"Consider how Michael Eisner, the CEO . . ."*
John Huey, "Secrets of Great Second Bananas," *Fortune,* May 6, 1991, pp. 64–76.

133   *"In 1953, the graduating class . . ."*
Don Wallace, "The Power of Goals," *Success,* September 1991, p. 43.

134   *"This purposeful commitment . . ."*
Mihaly Csikszentmihalyi, *Flow: The Psychology of Optimal Experience* (New York: Harper & Row, 1990).

146   *"For example, at Federal Express . . ."*
Brian Dumaine, "Who Needs a Boss?" *Fortune,* May 7, 1990, pp. 52–60.

7. How Followers Weave a Web of Relationships

PAGE

149   *"The term 'commons' dates back . . ."*
Garrett Hardin and John Baden, *Managing the Commons* (San Francisco: W. H. Freeman, 1977).

Notes

150   *"For example, in 1987 declining . . ."*
  Robert E. Kelley, "In Praise of Followers," *Harvard Business Review,* November–December 1988, pp. 142–48.
162   *"When disagreeing with the leader . . ."*
  Some of this material also appeared in an article for which Richard Greene interviewed me. See Richard Greene, "Seven Steps to Winning a Fight," *Forbes,* July 25, 1988, pp. 200–1.
165   *"Edward R. Murrow summed it up . . ."*
  L. J. Peter, *Peter's Quotations: Ideas for Our Time* (New York: Morrow, 1977).
166   *"They echo Paderewski, the famous . . ."*
  James C. Humes, *Speaker's Treasury of Anecdotes About the Famous* (New York: Barnes & Noble, 1978).

8. The Courageous Conscience

PAGE
170   *"As Stanford psychologist Phil Zimbardo . . ."*
  P. Zimbardo, "Psychology Today: The State of the Science," *Psychology Today,* May 1982, pp. 63–65.
  Joan Hamilton, "Zimbardo," *Stanford Managing,* September 1990, pp. 30–35.
  Stanley Milgram's classic studies of obedience highlighted people's tendency to compromise their principles in the face of authority. See Stanley Milgram, *Obedience to Authority: An Experimental View* (New York: Harper, 1974).
171   *"According to Bill Frederick . . ."*
  Rick Wartzman, "Nature or Nurture? Study Blames Ethical Lapses on Corporate Goals," *Wall Street Journal,* October 9, 1987, p. 27.
  William Frederick and Lee Preston, *Business Ethics: Research Issues and Empirical Studies* (Greenwich, Conn.: JAI Press, 1990).
  William Frederick and James Weber, "The Values of Corporate Managers and Their Critics: An Empirical Description and Normative Implications," in ibid.
171   *"After analyzing ten studies . . ."*
  Wartzman, loc. cit.
171   *"For example, M. Cash Matthews . . ."*
  M. Cash Matthews, "Codes of Ethics: Organizational Behavior and Misbehavior," in Frederick and Preston, op. cit., pp. 99–122.
174   *"The ancients who wished . . ."*
  Bette Bao Lord, *Spring Moon* (New York: Avon, 1981).
175   *". . . focus primarily on their 'duty to obey' . . ."*
  Herbert C. Kelman and V. Lee Hamilton, *Crimes of Obedience* (New Haven: Yale University Press, 1989).

Notes

175   *". . . Art Fry had a new product idea . . ."*
       Gifford Pinchot, *Intrapreneuring* (New York: Harper & Row, 1985).
176   *"It helps us avoid what social ethicists . . ."*
       Kelman and Hamilton, op. cit.
180   *"In June 1987, a federal grand jury . . ."*
       J. Holusha, "Chrysler Acts in False Mileage Case," *New York
       Times,* July 2, 1987, pp. D1, D4.
181   *"For example, Scott Peck . . ."*
       M. Scott Peck, *People of the Lie* (New York: Simon & Schuster,
       1983).
183   *"As Thomas Jefferson said . . ."*
       Fawn M. Brodie, *Thomas Jefferson: An Intimate History* (New York:
       W. W. Norton, 1974).

9. Ten Steps to a Courageous Conscience

PAGE

186   *"Harvey Hornstein, a Columbia . . ."*
       Harvey Hornstein, *Managerial Courage* (New York: John Wiley &
       Sons, 1986).
186   *"This was clearly the case with Jerome LiCari . . ."*
       Chris Welles, "What Led Beech-Nut Down the Road to Disgrace,"
       Business Week, February 22, 1988, pp. 124–28.
       Morton Mintz, "Careers, Trust at Stake in Beech-Nut Trial," *Wash-
       ington Post,* November 29, 1987, p. 2.
187   *"As Hornstein concluded about . . ."*
       Hornstein, op. cit.
188   *"the single most important foundation . . ."*
       James Bond Stockdale, "The Principles of Leadership," *Education
       Digest,* 47 (March 1982), p. 24.
189   *"You're walking a very lonely road . . ."*
       John Huey, "Nothing is Impossible," *Fortune,* September 23, 1991,
       pp. 135–40.
191   *"We believe our first responsibility . . ."*
       Ted Tuleja, *Beyond the Bottom Line* (New York: Penguin Books,
       1985).
192   *"A lesser-known story involves . . ."*
       James Keogh, *Corporate Ethics: A Prime Business Asset* (New
       York: The Business Roundtable, February 1988).
192   *"When Art Fry was developing . . ."*
       Gifford Pinchot, *Intrapreneuring* (New York: Harper & Row, 1985).
192   *"Columbia's Harvey Hornstein . . ."*
       Hornstein, op. cit.
194   *"In the late 1970s . . ."*
       Pinchot, op. cit.

Notes

196   *"For example, a manager at Herman Miller . . ."*
       Max DePree, *Leadership Is an Art* (New York: Doubleday, 1989).
196   *"Jerome LiCari, the R&D manager . . ."*
       Mintz, op. cit.
       J. Holusha, "Chrysler Acts in False Mileage Case," *New York Times,* July 2, 1987, pp. D1, D4.

10. Leadership Secrets from Exemplary Followers

PAGE
199   *"You and I ought not to die . . ."*
       Fawn M. Brodie, *Thomas Jefferson: An Intimate History* (New York: W. W. Norton, 1974).
201   *"Based on my surveys, followers . . ."*
       Robert E. Kelley, "Gold-Collar Worker Survey," unpublished summary, Carnegie-Mellon University, 1990.
       Labor Letter, "Trust and Loyalty Run Low at American Companies," *Wall Street Journal,* January 16, 1990, p. A1.
       Carol Hymowitz, "Many Middle Managers Find Bosses Uninspiring," *Wall Street Journal,* November 6, 1989, p. B1.
204   *"When Hugh Aaron's closely held . . ."*
       Hugh Aaron, "In Troubled Times Run an Open Company," *Wall Street Journal,* December 10, 1990, p. A10.
206   *"If you want to solicit this information . . ."*
       Walter Kiechel III, "When Subordinates Evaluate the Boss," *Fortune,* June 19, 1989, pp. 201–2.
207   *"But Ed Lawler's extensive research . . ."*
       Edward E. Lawler, *High Involvement Management: Participative Strategies for Improving Organizational Performance* (San Francisco: Jossey-Bass, 1986).
       Edward E. Lawler, *Pay and Organization Development* (Reading, Mass.: Addison-Wesley, 1971).
       Edward E. Lawler, *Strategic Pay* (San Francisco: Jossey-Bass, 1990).
208   *"For example, a CEO of a furniture . . ."*
       Robert E. Kelley, *The Gold-Collar Worker* (Reading, Mass.: Addison-Wesley, 1985).
209   *"As Admiral James Stockdale . . ."*
       James Bond Stockdale, "The Principles of Leadership," *Education Digest,* 47 (March 1982), p. 24.
209   *"As Ilene Gochman of the . . ."*
       Alan Farnham, "The Trust Gap," *Fortune,* December 4, 1989, pp. 56–78.
209   *"[CEO pay] may be financed . . ."*
       Ibid.
210   *"When General Motors' profit slid . . ."*
       Carol Hymowitz, "More Employees, Shareholders Demand That

Notes

Sacrifices in Pay Begin at the Top," *Wall Street Journal*, November 8, 1990, pp. B1, B4.

210   *"One such leader is Ken Iverson . . ."*

Robert E. Kelley, *The Gold-Collar Worker* (Reading, Mass.: Addison-Wesley, 1985).

Farnham, op. cit.

213   *"Be less a hero . . ."*

Charles C. Manz and Henry P. Simms, Jr., *SuperLeadership* (New York: Prentice Hall, 1989).

"SuperLeadership: Beyond the Myth of Heroic Leadership," *Organizational Dynamics*, Spring 1991, pp. 18–35.

216   *"Dean Ruwe, president of . . ."*

Michael A. Verespej, "Partnership in the Trenches," *Industry Week*, October 17, 1988, pp. 56–64.

224   *"Sociologist A. W. Gouldner . . ."*

A. W. Gouldner, "Cosmopolitans and Locals: Toward an Analysis of Latent Social Roles—I & II," *Administrative Science Quarterly*, 2 (1957, 1958).

225   *"On a different level . . ."*

John Pfeiffer, "The Secret of Life at the Limits: Cogs Become Big Wheels," *Smithsonian*, July 1989, pp. 38–48.

Postscript

PAGE

232   *"At the dock outside the plane terminal . . ."*

Jared Diamond, "The Price of Human Folly," *Discover*, April 1989, pp. 73–77.

234   *". . . act without leaders . . ."*

For a recent discussion of various alternatives to leadership, see Jon P. Howell, David E. Bowen, Peter W. Dorfman, Steven Kerr, and Philip M. Podsakoff, "Substitutes for Leadership: Effective Alternatives to Ineffective Leadership," *Organizational Dynamics*, Summer 1990, pp. 21–38.

235   *Vaclav Havel: Or, Living in Truth,* edited by Jan Vladislav (London: Faber & Faber, 1986).

Bibliography

Hugh Aaron, "In Troubled Times Run an Open Company," *Wall Street Journal,* December 10, 1990, p. A10.

Claire Ansberry and Peter Pae, "Kodak's Cost-Cutting Bid Brings Yawn on Wall Street but Concern in Hometown," *Wall Street Journal,* August 25, 1989, p. A4.

Gideon Argov, "Recessions Create Opportunities—If You Break the Rules," *Wall Street Journal,* January 7, 1991, p. A14.

Aristotle, *The Politics,* edited by Stephen Everson (Cambridge, Eng.: Cambridge University Press, 1988).

Arnold "Red" Auerbach, "Misleading Followers," *Harvard Business Review,* January–February 1989, p. 152.

F. G. Bailey, *Humbuggery and Manipulation* (Ithaca, N.Y.: Cornell University Press, 1988).

Jonathan Barnes, *Aristotle.* (Oxford: Oxford University Press, 1982).

Amanda Bennet, "When Money Is Tight, Bosses Scramble for Other Ways to Motivate the Troops," *Wall Street Journal,* October 31, 1990, pp. B1, B9.

Warren Bennis, *On Becoming a Leader* (Reading, Mass.: Addison-Wesley, 1989).

———, "When There Are Too Many Chiefs," *Industry Week,* May 15, 1989, pp. 34–36.

———, *Why Leaders Can't Lead: The Unconscious Conspiracy Continues* (San Francisco: Jossey-Bass, 1989).

Nathaniel Branden, *Judgment Day: My Years with Ayn Rand* (Boston: Houghton Mifflin, 1989).

Fawn M. Brodie, *Thomas Jefferson: An Intimate History* (New York: Norton, 1974).

William Broyles, Jr., *Brothers in Arms: A Journey from War to Peace* (New York: Alfred A. Knopf, 1986).

M. C. Brown, "Administration Succession and Organizational Performance: The Succession Effect," *Administrative Science Quarterly,* 29 (1982), pp. 245–73.

James MacGregor Burns, *Leadership* (New York: Harper & Row, 1978).

Greg Bustin, "What to Do When You Suddenly Become the Chief," *Wall Street Journal,* October 31, 1988, p. A16.

Philip Caputo, *A Rumor of War* (New York: Holt, Rinehart and Winston, 1977).

Ronald B. Cohen, "Good Employees Are Easy to Keep If They're Happy at Their Work," *The Plain Dealer,* August 6, 1991.

Bibliography

Mihaly Csikszentmihalyi, *Flow: The Psychology of Optimal Experience* (New York: Harper & Row, 1990).

Dante, *Inferno*, translated by Mark Musa (Bloomington: Indiana University Press, 1971).

Allen F. Davis, *American Heroine: The Life and Legend of Jane Addams* (New York: Oxford University Press, 1973).

David Day and Robert Lord, "Executive Leadership and Organizational Performance," *Journal of Management*, 14 (September 1988), p. 453.

Max DePree, *Leadership Is an Art* (New York: Doubleday, 1989).

Jared Diamond, "The Price of Human Folly," *Discover*, April 1989, pp. 73–77.

Linda Donn, *Freud and Jung: Years of Friendship, Years of Loss* (New York: Scribner's, 1988).

Peter Drucker, "Permanent Cost Cutting," *Wall Street Journal*, January 11, 1991, p. A10.

Brian Dumaine, "Who Needs a Boss?" *Fortune*, May 7, 1990, pp. 52–60.

Alan Farnham, "The Trust Gap," *Fortune*, December 4, 1989, pp. 56–78.

Selwyn Feinstein, "Trust and Loyalty Run Low at American Companies," *Wall Street Journal*, January 16, 1990, p. A1.

Richard P. Feynman, *Surely You're Joking, Mr. Feynman!* (New York: Bantam, 1986).

William C. Frederick, *Business & Society* (New York: McGraw-Hill, 1988).

William C. Frederick and Lee Preston, *Business Ethics: Research Issues and Empirical Studies* (Greenwich, Conn.: JAI Press, 1990).

William C. Frederick and James Weber, "The Values of Corporate Managers and Their Critics: An Empirical Description and Normative Implications," in William C. Frederick and Lee Preston, *Business Ethics: Research Issues and Empirical Studies* (Greenwich, Conn.: JAI Press, 1990).

G. Ronald Gilbert, "Effective Leaders Must Be Good Followers Too," *Government Executive*, June 1990, p. 58.

G. Ronald Gilbert and Albert C. Hyde, "Followership and the Federal Worker," *Public Administration Review*, November–December 1988, pp. 962–68.

Lawrence G. Gipson, *The Coming of the Revolution* (New York: Harper & Row, 1954).

Daniel Goleman, "Agreeable or Anger," *New York Times Magazine*, April 16, 1989, p. 20.

A. W. Gouldner, "Cosmopolitans and Locals: Toward an Analysis of Latent Social Roles—I & II," *Administrative Science Quarterly*, 2 (1957, 1958).

Ellen Graham, "McDonald's Pickle: He Began Fast Food but Gets No Credit," *Wall Street Journal*, August 15, 1991, p. A1.

Richard Greene, "Seven Steps to Winning a Fight," *Forbes*, July 25, 1988, pp. 200–1.

Joan Hamilton, "Zimbardo," *Stanford Magazine*, September 1990, pp. 30–35.

Harry Harding, *Organizing China: The Problem of Bureaucracy 1949–1976* (Stanford, Calif.: Stanford University Press, 1981).

Bibliography

Vaclav Havel: Or, Living in Truth, edited by Jan Vladislav (London: Faber & Faber, 1986).

H. R. Hays, ed., *Bertolt Brecht: Selected Poems* (New York: Harcourt Brace Jovanovich, 1974).

G. W. F. Hegel, *The Philosophy of Hegel,* edited by Carl J. Friedrich (New York: Modern Library, 1953).

J. Holusha, "Chrysler Acts in False Mileage Case," *New York Times,* July 2, 1987, pp. D1, D9.

Harvey A. Hornstein, *Managerial Courage* (New York: Wiley, 1986).

Jon P. Howell, David E. Bowen, Peter W. Dorfman, Steven Kerr, and Philip M. Podsakoff, "Substitutes for Leadership: Effective Alternatives to Ineffective Leadership," *Organizational Dynamics,* Summer 1990, pp. 21–38.

John Huey, "Nothing Is Impossible," *Fortune,* September 23, 1991, pp. 135–40.

———, "Secrets of Great Second Bananas," *Fortune,* May 6, 1991, pp. 64–76.

James C. Humes, *Speaker's Treasury of Anecdotes about the Famous* (New York: Barnes & Noble, 1978).

Carol Hymowitz, "Many Middle Managers Find Bosses Uninspiring," *Wall Street Journal,* November 6, 1989, p. B1.

———, "More Employees, Shareholders Demand That Sacrifices in Pay Begin at the Top," *Wall Street Journal,* November 8, 1990, pp. B1, B4.

Robert E. Kelley, "Combining Followership and Leadership into Partnership," in *Making Organizations Competitive,* edited by R. Kilmann, I. Kilmann, et al. (San Francisco: Jossey-Bass, 1991).

———, "Followers Make the Leader," *Los Angeles Times,* November 19, 1988, Part II, p. 8.

———, *The Gold-Collar Worker* (Reading, Mass.: Addison-Wesley, Inc., 1985).

———, "Gold-Collar Worker Survey," unpublished summary, Carnegie-Mellon University, 1990.

———, "In Praise of Followers," *Harvard Business Review,* November–December 1988, pp. 142–48.

———, "A Society Can Succeed If It Has Effective Followers," *Chicago Tribune,* October 26, 1988, Section 1, p. 22.

Herbert C. Kelman and V. Lee Hamilton, *Crimes of Obedience* (New Haven: Yale University Press, 1989).

Donald Kennedy, "Learning, Thinking, Believing," *Stanford Magazine,* September 1990, pp. 27–29.

James Keogh, *Corporate Ethics: A Prime Business Asset* (New York: The Business Roundtable, February 1988).

Walter Kiechel III, "The Case Against Leaders," *Fortune,* November 21, 1988, pp. 217–20.

———, "When Subordinates Evaluate the Boss," *Fortune,* June 19, 1989, pp. 201–2.

Bibliography

David Kirkpatrick, "How the Workers Run Avis Better," *Fortune*, December 5, 1988, pp. 103–14.

E. A. Kracke, Jr., "Family vs. Merit in Chinese Civil Service Examinations under the Empire," in *Studies of Governmental Institutions in Chinese History*, edited by John L. Bishop (Cambridge, Mass.: Harvard University Press, 1968), pp. 171–94.

Edward E. Lawler, *High Involvement Management: Participative Strategies for Improving Organizational Performance* (San Francisco: Jossey-Bass, 1986).

———, *Pay and Organization Development* (Reading, Mass.: Addison-Wesley, 1971).

———, *Strategic Pay* (San Francisco: Jossey-Bass, 1990).

S. Lieberson and J. F. O'Connor, "Leadership and Organizational Performance: A Study of Large Corporations," *American Sociological Review*, 37 (1972), pp. 117–30.

William Litzinger and Thomas Schaefer, "Leadership Through Followership," *Business Horizons*, September–October 1982, pp. 78–81.

Bette Bao Lord, *Spring Moon* (New York: Avon, 1981).

Michael E. McGill, *American Business and the Quick Fix* (New York: Henry Holt, 1988).

Charles C. Manz and Henry P. Sims, Jr., "Leading Workers to Lead Themselves: The External Leadership of Self-Managing Work Teams," *Administrative Science Quarterly*, 32 (1987), pp. 106–28.

———, *SuperLeadership* (New York: Prentice Hall, 1989).

———, "SuperLeadership: Beyond the Myth of Heroic Leadership," *Organizational Dynamics*, Spring 1991, pp. 18–35.

M. Cash Matthews, "Codes of Ethics: Organizational Behavior and Misbehavior," in William Fredericks and Lee Preston, *Business Ethics: Research Issues and Empirical Studies* (Greenwich, Conn.: JAI Press, 1990), pp. 99–122.

James R. Meindl, Sanford B. Ehrlich, and Janet M. Dukerich, "The Romance of Leadership," *Administrative Science Quarterly*, 30 (1985), pp. 78–102.

Morton Mintz, "Careers, Trust at Stake in Beech-Nut Trial," *Washington Post*, November 29, 1987, p. H2.

Stanley J. Modic, "Whatever It Is, It's Not Working," *Industry Week*, July 17, 1989, p. 27.

James Morgan, "Fifty Ways to Lose Your Languor," *American Way*, August 15, 1991, pp. 57–83.

———, "Wily Varmints," *Investment Vision*, June–July 1991, pp. 64–69.

Inazo Nitobe, *Bushido: The Soul of Japan* (Rutland, Vt.: Charles E. Tuttle, 1969).

Dean Ornish, *Dr. Dean Ornish's Program for Reversing Heart Disease* (New York: Random House, 1990).

Edward C. Page, *Political Authority and Bureaucratic Power: A Comparative Analysis* (Knoxville: University of Tennessee Press, 1985).

M. Scott Peck, *People of the Lie* (New York: Simon & Schuster, 1983).

Bibliography

L. J. Peter, *Peter's Quotation: Ideas for Our Time* (New York: Morrow, 1977).

J. Pfeffer, "The Ambiguity of Leadership," *Academy of Management Review,* 2 (1977), 104–12.

John Pfeiffer, "The Secret of Life at the Limits: Cogs Become Big Wheels," *Smithsonian,* July 1989, pp. 38–48.

Gifford Pinchot, III, *Intrapreneuring* (New York: Harper & Row, 1985).

G. R. Salancik and J. Pfeffer, "Constraints on Administrative Discretion: The Limited Influence of Mayors on City Budgets," *Urban Affairs Quarterly,* 12 (1977), pp. 474–98.

J. D. Salinger, *Franny and Zooey* (Boston: Little, Brown, 1961).

Duane Schultz, *Intimate Friends, Dangerous Rivals: The Turbulent Relationship Between Freud and Jung* (Los Angeles: Jeremy P. Tarcher, 1990).

Jeff Sewald, "A Writer's Life," *Pittsburgh Magazine,* July 1991, pp. 24–46.

James Stockdale, "The Principles of Leadership," *Education Digest,* 47 (March 1982), p. 24.

Irving Stone, *The Passions of the Mind* (New York: Doubleday, 1971).

Ssu-Yu Teng, "Chinese Influence on the Western Examination System," in *Studies of Governmental Institutions in Chinese History,* edited by John L. Bishop (Cambridge, Mass.: Harvard University Press, 1968), pp. 195–242.

Ted Tuleja, *Beyond the Bottom Line* (New York: Penguin, 1985).

Michael A. Verespej, "Partnership in the Trenches," *Industry Week,* October 17, 1988, pp. 56–64.

Don Wallace, "The Power of Goals," *Success,* September 1991, p. 43.

Rick Wartzman, "Nature or Nurture? Study Blames Ethical Lapses on Corporate Goals," *Wall Street Journal,* October 9, 1987, p. 27.

Dale Wasserman, *Man of La Mancha* (New York: Random House, 1966).

Chris Welles, "What Led Beech-Nut Down the Road to Disgrace," *Business Week,* February 22, 1988, pp. 124–28.

Alden Whitman, *American Reformers* (New York: H. W. Wilson, 1985).

Wang Yu-Chuan, "An Outline of the Central Government of the Former Han Dynasty," in *Studies of Governmental Institutions in Chinese History,* edited by John L. Bishop (Cambridge, Mass.: Harvard University Press, 1968), pp. 1–56.

Gary A. Yukl, *Leadership in Organizations* (Englewood Cliffs, N.J.: Prentice Hall, 1981, 1989).

Daidoji Yuzan, *The Code of the Samurai,* translated by A. L. Sadler (Rutland, Vt.: Charles E. Tuttle, 1941, 1988).

Abraham Zaleznik, "Managers and Leaders: Are They Different?" *Harvard Business Review,* May–June 1977, pp. 67–78.

William E. Zierden, "Leading Through the Followers' Point of View," *Organizational Dynamics,* Spring 1980, pp. 27–46.

P. Zimbardo, "Psychology Today: The State of the Science," *Psychology Today,* May 1982, pp. 63–68.

INDEX

Index

Index

Index